"Brilliant work! Integrates the 'new' world and the 'new' economic realities with the 'new' science and technologies, leaving the serious reader with an amazingly useful, principle-based dynamic framework of thinking. These two authors have achieved a remarkable synergy between them and also between the theoretical and the practical."

–Stephen Covey, best-selling author, *The 7 Habits of Highly Effective People*

"This is good stuff—an unbelievable amount of new observations and connections. The lessons drawn from modern science are the best I've seen anywhere. The Ten Principles and 'key actions' the authors entail will be really valuable material for managers who sail into the teeth of complexity and paradox."

–Perry Pascarella, former editor-in-chief, *Industry Week*

"*Large-Scale Organizational Change* opens new and promising avenues for leaders of large organizations. It shows how ecological sustainability itself changes the relationship between business and the outside world. An exciting and thought-provoking book!"

–Bertrand Collomb, chairman and CEO, Lafarge S.A.

"This ambitious book is one of the first to link techniques and lessons from the new science to the emerging issues of environmental sustainability. Clearly written and interesting, it sounds the alarm about the long-term consequences of business actions."

–Larry Perlman, chairman and CEO, Ceridian Corporation

"This new work is a state-of-the-art look at leadership in large-scale organizations from the vantage of the new sciences of complexity and chaos theory. It clearly articulates the idea of continual reinvention or 'perpetual transformation,' the

main theme and special contribution of the book, that increasingly confronts executives in today's business climate. Building on other works published in this field—including Howard Sherman's own recent books and mine—Laszlo and Laugel stand out by their practical applications for large-scale companies. The Ten Principles and corresponding actions are useable guidelines for practicing executives. The authors' background experience as executives in Fortune 500 companies shows through in the writing. Their chapters on information management and environmental responsibility are natural extensions of the core approach and unique contributions to the field. The link the authors make between perpetual transformation and environmental sustainability is one of the first attempts to do so since Paul Hawken's *The Ecology of Commerce."*

–**Mike McMaster,** author, *The Intelligence Advantage* and *The Praxis Equation: Design Principles for Intelligent Organisation*

"Laszlo and Laugel have made complexity and chaos theory relevant for the school of hard knocks in this practical guide. As a change practitioner, I appreciate the 'real world' ring of experience that comes through in the text. 'Get results and keep the change!' should be the headline for the bestseller reviews!"

–**Don C. Hawley,** former president and CEO, Symmetrix, Inc.

"Large-Scale Organizational Change provides an extremely interesting new cut on the underlying trends in today's economy and a number of very useful principles for managers as they try to weather the storm. This book is a very timely addition to business literature. Its themes strike a chord within our organization for sure."

–**James Bond,** director, World Bank

"Laszlo and Laugel successfully translate revelations from the new sciences of quantum physics and chaos theory about the nature of reality into practical principles that managers can apply in day-to-day business. Large multinationals like Levi Strauss & Co. are too complex to operate without the principles of self-organization. The question is whether we will consciously utilize these principles—or be dominated by them. This book shows us how to be proactive in using them."

–**Tina Rasmussen,** senior global consultant, Levi Strauss & Co.

"This comprehensive review of organizations amalgamating the sciences of management, mathematics, biology, and history leads the way not only toward a new kind of management but a new kind of corporate reality. Making use of the methodology described in this book will allow companies to evolve to a state where they are able to adapt to any change of environment and maintain this capacity long term."

–**Jean-Marc Arbaud,** president, SNC–Lavalin Agriculture & Agrifund, Canada

"If you believe the only constant is change, then this book should be your guide for creating a management strategy that will be an exception to that rule."

–**Darrell Brown,** president and executive editor, *Leaders* magazine

"*Large-Scale Organizational Change* defines the new mode for multinational organizations facing constant challenges and intense global competition. 'High fives' for both authors for providing a lifesaver for the courageous sailors of the big ships that dare these incredible times."

–**John E. Renesch,** editor, *Learning Organizations* and *Leadership in a New Era*

"As organizations struggle through confusing times, the new sciences of complexity and chaos offer special help. Laszlo and Laugel skillfully integrate this body of knowledge and practical examples with their management experience in guiding corporate transformation."

–**William E. Halal,** author, *The New Management*, and management professor, George Washington University

"Drawing on the developing sciences of complexity and chaos, the authors provide ten key principles for achieving effective and permanent transformation. Their executive positions and consulting experience with the world's most successful organizations—combined with strong academic backgrounds—allows them to provide a comprehensive set of guidelines for developing and executing an organization's strategic intent. Those concerned with the practice or study of this subject should definitely read what they have to say."

–**J. Randolph New,** dean, University of Richmond Business School

Large-Scale
Organizational Change

Large-Scale Organizational Change:

An Executive's Guide

CHRISTOPHER LASZLO

JEAN-FRANÇOIS LAUGEL

Boston, Oxford, Auckland, Johannesburg, Melbourne, New Delhi

Library of Congress Cataloging-in-Publication Data
Laszlo, Christopher.
    Large scale organizational change: an executive's guide / Christopher Laszlo, Jean-François Laugel.
        p.   cm.
    ISBN 0-7506-7230-7 (paperback: alk. paper)
    1. Organizational change.   I. Laugel, Jean-François.   II. Title.
HD58.8.L377   1999
658.4'06—dc21   99-40495
                                                                      CIP

British Library Cataloguing-in-Publication Data
A catalogue record for this book is available from the British Library.

The publisher offers special discounts on bulk orders of this book.
For information, please contact:

Manager of Special Sales
Butterworth–Heinemann
225 Wildwood Avenue
Woburn, MA 01801–2041
Tel: 781-904-2500
Fax: 781-904-2620

For information on all Butterworth–Heinemann publications available, contact our World Wide Web home page at: http://www.bh.com

10 9 8 7 6 5 4 3 2 1

Printed in the United States of America

To
Lakshmi, Jenna, and Ishana
Françoise, Thibault, and Raphael

Contents

Preface   *xiii*
Acknowledgments   *xix*

Chapter 1   A New Wisdom   1

Chapter 2   Oracle and Lafarge: Perpetual
             Transformation in Action   7

Chapter 3   Chaos Dynamics: Lessons from the
             New Sciences   23

Chapter 4   The Ten Principles   35

Chapter 5   Principle I. Create Adaptive
             Strategies   43

Chapter 6   Principle II. Maintain Long-term
             Identity while Repositioning   55

Chapter 7   Principle III. Compete for Industry
             Sustainability   63

Chapter 8   Principle IV. Use Strategic
             Inflection Points   69

Chapter 9   Principle V. Link Transformation to
             Shareholder Value Creation   79

Chapter 10   Principle VI. Develop Ambitions
             Greater than Means   87

Chapter 11   Principle VII. Design Decision-
             making Systems for Self-
             organization   93

Chapter 12   Principle VIII. Fluidify the
Organizational Structure   107

Chapter 13   Principle IX. Use Organizational
Instability to Catalyze Learning   115

Chapter 14   Principle X. Reenvision Leading:
From Command and Control to
R(E)volutionary Influence   123

Chapter 15   Managing Information: A Key to
Successful Implementation   131

Chapter 16   Environmental Sustainability: An
Extension of the Ten Principles   159

Chapter 17   Conclusion   183

Appendix 1   *The New Corporate Reality*   *187*

Appendix 2   *Chaos Models in Business: Notes for the Technically
Minded*   *213*

Notes   *223*

Index   *227*

Preface

The purpose of this book is to provide a set of practical guidelines for managing change in complex and unstable environments. Companies faced with profound and ongoing change find themselves confronted with discontinuities and uncertainty in their operations. Among the most visible of these changes are globalization, e-commerce, the ever-increasing pace of technological innovation, shifting consumer values, and continued ecological problems linked to industry. Only by crafting a process of *perpetual transformation* can a company hope to survive, let alone have any chance of sustained financial performance. The guidelines in this book provide simple and clear keys to the whitewater world of business.

The management approaches that follow are the result of combining the latest insights available in the new sciences of complexity, chaos, and evolution with over 25 years of successful corporate experience with large-scale organizational change. The new sciences bring a conceptual framework to understanding the nature and dynamics of complexity, fluctuation, disorder, and uncertainty. The challenge in business has been to translate the new wisdom into guidelines for action. In seeking to meet this challenge, the authors have drawn on their own experience inside global industry leaders such as Lafarge (the world's largest construction materials company), Oracle (the third largest market capitalization in the software industry), and AXA-UAP (the world's number two insurance conglomerate). In addition, both authors worked as management consultants to companies such as Lucent Technologies, Toshiba, Avon Products, Rolls Royce, Campbell Soup, Agip, Renault, and DuPont on issues critical to strategy deployment.

Many executives in large organizations find themselves frustrated and confused by the seemingly never-ending bureaucracy and inertia in the face of turbulence and rapid change in the competitive environment. People who are otherwise creative and talented individuals become unwitting supporters of the status quo. Business units find themselves waiting for competitors to act first before making strategic decisions. Action recommendations are frequently met with a list of reasons why change is *not* possible. Action 1 will confuse traditional customers; Action 2 will cannibalize core products; Action 3 will require a different sales culture, and so on. In these kinds of organizations, resignation and loss of morale eventually overtake even the most enthusiastic new recruits.

Increasingly one hears that large multinationals are less fun places to work than small and mid-sized companies: stress levels are higher and job satisfaction is lower in large organizations, though salaries tend to be better. The *Financial Times* recently reported that out of 148 MBA students at the London School of Economics, only six aspired to management positions in established multinationals. The majority of students are looking for opportunities that will broaden and deepen their personal portfolio of skills, and that will allow them to contribute to society in ways that are more meaningful than can be achieved by working in a Fortune 500 company. "I think a lot more people are opting to go to work for smaller start-ups, maybe for the excitement and the chance to build something new. You have the chance to contribute more," says Rob Carney, a 1999 MBA graduate of the MIT Sloan School of Management.

This book seeks to make sense of large-scale organizations as living systems. Seeing the whole and understanding the dynamics of change in complex situations is fast becoming a business imperative for these companies. High performance is not only a question of being a good competitor; it requires being a good "evolver," i.e., possessing an awareness of the capabilities and culture that allows for change. In this awareness, complexity does not necessarily mean complicated or bureaucratic; chaos does not necessarily mean lack of order. "Managing" and "transformation" are not necessarily contradictory. And instability and turbulence are not to be avoided at all costs. The Ten Principles of Large Scale Organizational Change (LSOC), derived from the deeper laws of how living systems adapt and evolve, provide the reader with useful keys to managing in the new multinational corporate environment.

COMPLEXITY AND TURBULENCE: THE NEW ENVIRONMENT

In the realm of physics, it is now widely accepted that Newtonian laws, while relevant to the trajectory of mechanical objects in steady state environments, are not able to explain the so-called Brownian motion of electrons or the airflow of a jet engine through space. The new twentieth century science of Einstein, Hawking, Prigogine, Thom, and others came to incorporate phenomena such as relativity, uncertainty, instability, and chaos. Yet in management circles, the predominant schools of thought remain anchored in nineteenth century theory and practice. The "scientific management" of Frederick Taylor, and his later disciples Gantt and Gilbreth, have been refined and extended into ever more sophisticated models. Current variants include lean management (J. Womack, D. Jones), reengineering (M. Hammer, J. Champy), time-based management (T. Hout, G. Stalk), total quality management (E.W. Deming), industry and competitive value-chain analysis (M. Porter), shareholder value analysis (M. Rappaport), and a large number of tools and recipes promoted by gurus and management consulting firms. While all of these approaches are necessary, depending on competitive circumstances and management goals, none are sufficient in dealing with high present-day levels of complexity and instability.

The new competitive environment is qualitatively different from the one existing in previous decades. Within companies, the diffusion of information and the increase in number and intensity of interfaces between individuals, departments, and divisions, modify the way in which decisions are made. Information technology and configuration now heavily influence the process of productivity improvement. Internet companies are setting new rules in industries from bookselling to stock trading to how we buy a car. Externally, precise notions of where the company's activities end and where its environment begins have become vague. Activities previously considered essential are now subcontracted; networks of partnerships with other companies are extensive; and relations with suppliers and distributors are key competitive assets.

To this rapidly evolving landscape must be added emerging social and ecological constraints and opportunities. The ethical responsibility of executives in these areas is fast becoming a vital global issue. Leading corporate managers influence not only the survival of their companies and industries, but also the local communities and regional economies in which their companies operate. Their decisions affect not only the markets they serve but also the delicate ecologies in which they source, produce, and sell their goods and services. The way in which this responsibility is exercised will determine whether a company and industry will contribute toward a sustainable market, and whether its influence will be self-determined or regulated by government sanctions and penalties.

Throughout the book, our main focus remains on creating sustainable value for the stakeholders of the company including (but not limited to) shareholders, customers, and employees. Far from suggesting a conflict between creative and ethical behavior on the one hand, and short-term financial performance on the other, *Large-Scale Organizational Change* offers a way to achieve extraordinary results in complex and turbulent environments. It provides an emerging insight into the universal challenge of good management.

Christopher LASZLO
Great Falls, Virginia
July, 1999

Jean-François LAUGEL
Paris, France

Acknowledgments

Large-Scale Organizational Change is the integration and distillation of experience and thinking across a wide range of companies, individuals, and disciplines. We are deeply grateful to the executives, friends, colleagues, and employees who have shared their learning and influenced this book along the way. The list includes hundreds of managers with whom we have worked or consulted in this area, and who gave of their time to explore our ideas and put them into practice.

While we alone bear responsibility for what is said here, especially any errors or omissions, we wish to thank a small list of those people who have most influenced us and shaped the views expressed in this book. They are:

Dr. Ervin Laszlo, Prof. Pierre Grou, Duncan Gage, Don Hawley, Bertrand Collomb, Georges-Yves Kervern, Ray Deck, Jr., Serge Feneuille, Peter Roche, Dr. Solange Perret, Carita Laszlo, Dr. Alex Laszlo, Bill Mundell, and Ray Lane.

Special thanks to Karen Speerstra and Rita Lombard, our editors at Butterworth–Heinemann. Their engagement and creativity were part of a seamless effort to pull everything together in the project's final phases. We also wish to acknowledge John Renesch for his developmental editing and packaging efforts, and his persistence in getting the style of writing to reflect our intended readership.

Finally, our deepest thanks and love to our families. This book is dedicated to them.

Chapter 1

A New Wisdom

Hardly anyone in any boardroom around the world would not agree that the speed and complexity of change have reached dizzying proportions. Words like *chaotic* and *tumultuous* have become part of the everyday business lexicon. The urgency and rapid pace of everything have caused business thinkers to wonder where, or even whether, it will all sort out. Leading commentators are calling the situation "out of control."

The challenge of big business is to take advantage of complexity and turbulence rather than be overwhelmed by them. A company that meets this challenge would be excellent at providing customer value added at the lowest cost *and* would be able to adapt and sustain itself at the edge of chaos.

THE SEARCH FOR WISDOM

As our world becomes more complex and information increases with seemingly endless acceleration, executives and managers are seeking as much wisdom as possible for coping with this ever-increasing scale of change. They don't need more information. There is a virtual glut of knowledge. What is needed is wisdom—or what to do with all the knowledge.

Wisdom is produced when learning occurs, and learning happens when executives are willing to look at new sources of learning. Science has traditionally been a reliable source of wisdom about how the world works. The physics of Newton and biology of Darwin played strong roles in shaping our notions of economics and business. Those early sciences were the foundations of the executive learning inspired by Frederick Taylor in the early decades of the twentieth century. Efficiencies were gained through a rigorous application of "scientific management" that fueled the mass-production techniques of Henry Ford and the large-scale organization of Alfred Sloan's General Motors.

More recent advances in the so-called new sciences represent a rich reservoir of wisdom for managers and executives charged with the responsibility of leading large-scale organizations. This new wisdom includes lessons from nature about how highly adaptive living systems can grow and thrive despite seemingly chaotic influences. There are ever-increasing parallels between the realms of living systems in nature, in which chaos and complexity are everyday occurrences, and the business world. The global enterprise is buffeted by an endless stream of instantaneous financial transactions, competitor moves, unpredictable market events, and fickle social trends that play on profitability. Commerce has become a complex adaptive system in its own right. It simply is no longer realistic to manage a global corporation as if it were a simple clock mechanism to be taken apart, cleaned, oiled, and put back together to "run on time."

Many of the best insights into how organizations adapt and survive despite seemingly chaotic influences come to us from recent scientific discoveries in the behavior of living systems—from single-cell bacteria to the Brazilian wetlands. The lessons they teach us are very different from those mastered in business, in which management traditionally relies on engineered, controllable, hierarchical, analytical approaches. The new science is rich in metaphors: a butterfly flapping its wings, the neural networks of the brain, and the flocking behavior of geese. However, as soon as these living systems are reduced to their component systems—the brain to its neurons for example—their essential properties are lost. Executives confronted with this irreducible nature of complex living systems are intrigued by the new body of knowledge but frustrated in knowing what to do about it. The challenge is to translate the insights of the new science into useful knowledge—into business wisdom for managers with day-to-day accountabilities.

THE ARENA OF THE NEW SCIENCE

A new executive literacy is being called for in business. This new literacy requires executives to examine their primary assumptions about how things work and to adventure into new worlds of ideas, new vistas for creative leadership, new world views about reality. In response to this need, several excellent books have been written about complex living systems in a business context. Most, however, have been written from the perspective of the scientist, the theorist, and the academic. We wrote this book about the enormous value of the new sciences from the point of view of the executives, chief executive officers, strategic planners, and line managers who have responsibility for the ongoing sustainability of their companies.

BRIDGING THE GAP BETWEEN BUSINESS AND SCIENCE

In this book, we focus on two challenges and two accompanying promises. The first challenge and promise are to prescribe a "new science" version of strategy, organization, and leadership in business. This version must enable global companies to turn chaos and turbulence from a threat to survival into an opportunity for growth and profitability. The other challenge and promise are to bridge the gap between the language of management—the pragmatic mind-set and vocabulary of the business executive—and the language of science.

PERPETUAL TRANSFORMATION

The only successful way of surviving and adapting to chaos and complexity is to strive for perpetual transformation—that is the essential premise of this book. The pages that follow describe a process of continual reinvention whereby global companies transform themselves as their environments change. The transformation makes them highly adaptive in the complex market systems in which they operate and eliminate the need for periodic episodes of traumatic reinvention or painful and sometimes fatal reengineering.

The complex adaptive systems version of strategy, organization, and leadership enables managers to do the following:

- Achieve extraordinary business results
- Shape the future of the company
- Unleash the full creative potential of employees
- Integrate unpredictable change
- Contribute to global sustainability

Leading in complex environments involves an ongoing process in which the company continually reinvents itself, seeking new hilltops in the ever-changing competitive landscape. As companies face the information-rich competitive environment of the new millennium, past rules of success become obsolete. Links to a company's historical positioning and performance are discontinuous. The new leadership is more concerned with the ability to anticipate, the capacity to learn, opportunity-driven growth, inflection points, adaptive organization, knowledge generation, and the emergence of organizational intelligence than it is with hierarchy, authority, and control.

The transformation we imply is exhaustive. It includes the strategy, the organization, and the leadership style of the company. We use the term *transformation* to mean a process of altering context. The alteration reinvents the company. It is like the transformation of a chrysalis into a butterfly. A butterfly is not a new and improved pupa; it has fundamentally changed its existence. Transformation alters the essential nature and context of a company. In the process it allows an organization to create something that is not possible in its present reality.

Unlike the chrysalis-to-butterfly example, when it comes to the corporate world, transformation is not determined by a genetic code. The act of management provides an element of choice. In most large organizations, however, the choice is heavily biased toward perpetuating the status quo. Individuals and organizations typically work inside existing frameworks and apply formulas that have succeeded in the past. The greater the threat of change, the harder they try to adapt the present. The problem arises when existing frameworks and formulas for winning become irrelevant to a particular business situation. If a butterfly is called for, it simply does not make sense to improve the design and function of a chrysalis. Profound problems, Albert Einstein once said, cannot be solved from the same consciousness that created them.

The essence of perpetual transformation can be easily described: it would tap into the distributed intelligence of the entire organization and allow for the emergence of new strategies, structures, processes, and practices. Actions would no longer be planned by a few executives at the top with a golden touch at predicting and controlling. Instead business solutions would emerge from organizational learning, the alignment and coordination of individual actions, and the workings of informal knowledge communities. The full passion, spirit, and commitment of the organization would be brought to bear in the process. A shared culture of reinvention would exist in which everyone actively participates in creating a new and desirable future. The visible result would be the continuously emerging organization capable of sustaining itself indefinitely.

In the chapters that follow we provide a bridge that spans the chasm that separates the worlds of business and the new science. We stand on the shoulders of the people who have advanced some of these ideas and of executives with whom we have worked and who intuitively understood what the new leadership is all about.

Combining the latest insights of the new science with more than twenty-five years of successful corporate experience in managing change, we link the two disciplines so that lessons can travel freely from one to the other. The new wisdom will be that of business leaders acting decisively in seemingly complex and chaotic environments without having to experience the feeling that things are always "out of control."

Chapter 2

Oracle and Lafarge: Perpetual Transformation in Action

Here we illustrate the kind of results that have been obtained with perpetual transformation. A key point is that in these and similar applied cases, the approach is used knowingly *or unknowingly*. Intuition, experience, and knowledge all come into play in shaping the strategy and tactics of large-scale organizational change. In the following illustrations, articulated knowledge of the process of transformation played an important role in the successful management of change, even if intuition, experience, and luck were present. Wise use of knowledge to augment the business's likelihood of success is the main objective of good management.

The first example—Oracle Corporation—is drawn from the fast-moving world of high technology. This is a case of profound transformation over a four-year period in an unpredictable, competitive environment in which the future almost all the time is unrelated to the past. It deals with a globally successful industry leader that has repeatedly demonstrated a capability for reinventing itself. Oracle has maintained its leadership *because of* profound changes it has initiated for itself and its industry, not in spite of such changes.

The second example—Lafarge S.A.—is drawn from the more conservative, capital-intensive world of heavy industry. The case concerns the redesign of the $250 million cement division of Lafarge Corporation (U.S.) which had been under-performing during a prolonged down-market. In spite of low growth, poor economic conditions, and some industry over-capacity in the region covered, Lafarge was able to implement a multiyear transformation program that yielded immediate and significant results to the bottom line.

ORACLE: MANAGING HIGH-PERFORMANCE GROWTH

September 1998. A new organization is announced at Oracle. For the first time in the history of the database company, the organization acknowledges new sources of revenue for the firm outside database and development tools. The new structure lines up two completely separate lines of business: the emerging software application business, which had grown from scratch to become the number two competitor worldwide, and a parallel business unit covering the original database system products and tools. This new structure has its dedicated sales and consulting forces. The old revenue structure and the corresponding organization no longer exist.

Easy to do? Easy to say definitely, but consider that the outcome resulted from a change process implemented over four years in a forty-thousand-employee company growing at forty percent per year. Four years were necessary to make it happen after two aborted initiatives. Difficult to accept internally? Certainly! In the weeks that followed the announcement, key executives of the original Oracle submitted their resignations. Since then, however, the stock has continued its upward flight.

The Oracle story is hardly over. A culture of perpetual transformation, as is the case with many leading high-tech companies, from Intel to Lucent Technologies and Microsoft, is firmly in place. This slice of history is a particularly vivid illustration of corporate reinvention. Here is how it all happened.

With more than $8 billion in sales and nearly forty thousand employees, Oracle remains the global leader in database management systems and one of the world's largest software producers. Market valuation of close to $50 billion recently placed Oracle second among information technology stocks. As a company, Oracle is known primarily for its innovative database management software products, which range from third-generation development tools to application add-ons. Oracle also is regularly recognized by the national and international news media for its trend-setting industry leadership, particularly since 1996, when founder and chief executive officer Larry Ellison began his crusade for networking computers as a way to rival Bill Gates at Microsoft. Oracle achieved early success by positioning itself in the management of information and UNIX technology.

In recent years, companies in a broad range of industries have fought their rivals and won in terms of electronic information management. The discovery of new consumer needs based on data management has spanned the gamut from production systems to consumer services. These needs have required, from a technical point of view, new tools for data storage, classification, referencing, and retrieval. Such tools are generally known as relational database management systems (RDBMS). As the needs of industry in this area exploded, the global market for RDBMS grew exponentially.

Meanwhile, UNIX technology quickly overtook the dominant computer architecture that existed at the time, that of very large-scale centralized systems. Developed initially in the research laboratories of AT&T, UNIX provided an architecture that was better distributed between servers and between client workstations and servers. It allowed more flexible distribution of roles and tended to privilege the user in the process of accessing and analyzing information. The UNIX approach was popularized with the term *client-server.*

The explosive growth in its markets generated spectacular year-on-year earnings performance for Oracle. As the years passed, the range of products broadened while remaining highly technical in nature: information warehouses, database bridging software, development software, and general application software. A service offer was quickly added to this range of products: technical support for the installation of the software and adaptation to the specific needs of the client, which eventually involved fifteen thousand workers at Oracle, training on Oracle products, and a maintenance department.

The industrial expansion and financial performance of Oracle were sustained, except for a brief lag in 1991. That year a combination of macroeconomic recession and poor management led to a growing impasse, which the shareholders resolved with a change of leadership. Ray Lane was promoted to work at Larry Ellison's side, and a rebound began.

Ray Lane began by reorganizing the sales force, implementing standardized selling techniques, and paying commissions based on performance. He brought fresh impetus to product development and oversaw a dramatic increase in market share. From co-leader with Sybase in the domain of database management software, Oracle assumed a clear lead beginning in 1995.

The stock market performance of Oracle has been nothing short of spectacular. Ten thousand dollars invested in Oracle stock in 1986 would be worth more than $800,000 today, an eightyfold increase. In spite of sustained investor confidence, Lane saw clearly the need for the company to undergo profound and continuous transformation.

A few years after his nomination to the number two position in the company, Lane commissioned a six-person task force to propose and implement a transformation program to propel Oracle into being the partner of choice for large industrial customers in all facets of information management. One of the authors of this book (J.F.L.) was a senior director on that task force.

The Oracle Approach to Perpetual Transformation

The approach began with strategy formulation. This exercise was turned more toward the probable future than the statistical past. A wide-ranging assessment of trends and key business drivers was undertaken. Understanding clients, their needs and expectations, and the technologies available to satisfy those needs and expectations was an essential first step. It also was essential to understand how information-management technology could assist client organizations in establishing their own strategic inflection points as a way to differentiate themselves from the competition. The challenge for Oracle was to create discontinuities in information technology and systems that would allow users to create their own discontinuities in the operative environment. This challenge forced the entire organization to think in terms of probability-based scenarios and anticipated projects (of competitors, clients, covendors, and distributors) and to develop a deep, shared understanding from which aligned actions could be taken in an uncertain environment.

Proactive strategy formulation allowed Oracle to define the leading edge of user needs segmented according to client industry, such as banking, consumer goods, pharmaceuticals, and oil and gas. Such segmentation allowed Oracle to evaluate where it had the greatest potential for sales. In some industry sectors it could expect to be a leader and in others a strong outsider. In other areas the nature of the business did not merit the effort. A first cut revealed four target industries, each requiring its own strategy.

Because the world of information management evolves rapidly and in a discontinuous way, industry-specific strategies required sufficient flexibility and openness to allow new and unplanned developments, whether internal or external. It was soon learned that external events had to be integrated on an ongoing basis, as illustrated by the mergers and acquisitions of this period (e.g., PeopleSoft and RedPepper, IBM and Lotus).

Once the target industries and strategies were given shape, the next step was to work out the value-added offer and target client companies. New questions arose at this stage, such as whether the value-added offers should come exclusively from Oracle teams or whether it would be more effective to combine in-house products with potential partners and their products. It was decided to open the process to outside vendors, a decision akin to seeking coevolutionary partnerships (see Chapter 7) within the industry. A program to select and grow covendor relationships was developed and called Industry Solution Initiative (ISI).

With their new products and services focused on the future needs of industry-specific clients, Oracle and its partners were able to become the supplier of choice for large companies looking to use information management as a means to create successful discontinuities in their own businesses. To steer the process over time, a precise but flexible piloting system was put in place.

The transformation process undertaken by Oracle in an extremely complex and turbulent environment allowed continued client satisfaction and shareholder value creation. It required changing a winning formula, a process of selectively forgetting the past, in spite of a forty percent per year growth rate in earnings that each given formula had produced. Altering a winning formula takes courage and vision in the face of high levels of uncertainty.

Throughout the process, the top management of Oracle was never forced to create its own instabilities. The competitive environment produced sufficient inflection points to maintain creativity and learning. The rhythm of change in the external environment allowed a much more condensed form of transformation than is typically possible in low-tech and more stable industries.

The results produced during the 1990s were an outcome of a perfect coherence between strategy, organization, and execution. The coherence was assured by shareholder value measures and founded on satisfying current and future client needs. The changing organization of Oracle—from technical sales to system products for key accounts at the senior management level—could have happened only through a sustained transformation process.

Industry-specific Approaches

The Consumer Goods Industry

The consumer goods sector was targeted by Oracle as one in which competitive pressures on operating margins would force players to seek differentiation through information management throughout the value-added chain. The proposed solution to these margin pressures (Oracle Consumer Goods Products) provided an integrated sequence of in-house and outside vendor products. The sequence covered a client's entire operation from conception and purchases of raw materials to services for the ultimate user. This product allowed client companies to increase market share by increasing cycle times and targeting evolving user needs more efficiently.

In the consumer goods sector, the approach sought initially to improve database management and subsequently focused on add-on applications software such as financial management. Covendors included Manugistics for planning and procurement, TSW for maintenance, Matematik for order taking, and Datalogix for production in continuous series. Datalogix later was acquired by Oracle.

The Banking Industry

In the banking sector, Oracle initially developed a policy of covendor partnership to cover the broadest possible needs of the banking industry. A partner selection program was undertaken in the mid 1990s to identify the best overall solution and to persuade potential partners to join the Oracle offer. In January 1997, an announcement was made identifying one hundred eighty suppliers who had elected to participate in the Oracle partnership.

The Oracle offer included risk analysis, financial management, financial performance monitoring, and many other key functions undertaken by banks. Covendors were companies such as Broadway and Seymour, CATS Software, Corfax, FAME, Financial Technologies International, HNC Software, Infinity, Oasis, Premier Solutions, Princeton Financial, Summit, Super Solutions, Synopsis, TIBCO, and Treasury Services Corporation. Oracle concurrently developed a funds transfer and payment system for the Internet. This system included state-of-the-art security. It allowed Internet users to make purchases and pay instantaneously without concern for confidentiality or theft.

The Pharmaceutical Industry

In contrast to its effort in the banking sector, Oracle undertook a single-company approach (without any partners) to the pharmaceutical market. Players in this industry placed strong emphasis on the classification and follow-up procedures of clinical tests to obtain product certification and approval. Oracle developed a product specific to this need called Oracle Clinical.

The Oil and Gas Industry

The oil and gas industry also was subject to a single-company proprietary approach. Oracle acquired a series of software products that had been developed to meet internal information-management needs of oil and gas companies. For example, in June 1997, Oracle announced the purchase of the distribution software of British Petroleum. These products were intended for integration with exploration and oil-field management software to provide complete solutions in the sector. Integrated solutions will provide a basis for Oracle to serve the leading companies in key information-management areas.

LAFARGE CORPORATION: LARGE-SCALE CHANGE IN A CAPITAL-INTENSIVE MANUFACTURING BUSINESS

Lafarge S.A. is a $10 billion building materials company, the world's largest. It manufactures and sells cement, aggregates, ready-mix concrete, roofing products, gypsum board, and specialty chemicals in sixty countries. In 1998 Lafarge had more than sixty thousand employees. It also has a distinguished history. The company was founded in 1833 and has been consistently profitable for much of its existence. The events described concern a large division (since partially divested) that underwent sustained transformation with dramatic results over several years.

At the start of these events, the $250 million southern division of the U.S. subsidiary Lafarge Corporation was in poor shape. With average annual net losses of more than $10 million over the previous five years, it had slipped into a high-delivered-cost position in a commodity business. Although the division was essentially a single-product manufacturer (cement), its business was characterized by many different geographic markets, competitors, and customer groups. Environmental standards and community concerns also were becoming important factors. Added complexity came from the division's interface with other regional divisions of Lafarge Corporation, U.S. headquarters in Virginia, and world headquarters in Paris. It became apparent that what was needed was complete restructuring of the division's activities, including assets and contracts, sales and marketing, distribution, administration, and organization.

Previous efforts to execute effective change had failed for a number of reasons, including lack of capital funds and difficult economic conditions. The leadership also had limitations. Some local decisions had been made with negative consequences for the division as a whole, and some divisional decisions had not taken into account local conditions. Middle and lower managers had been largely excluded from decision making. An annual planning ritual produced more than two hundred pages of material but stifled creativity and action. It also remained far removed from the customer. The complexity of the business had paralyzed decision making within the existing organizational structure and its mode of operation.

As is often the case with global companies, attempts to resolve the growing impasse took the form of a search for "big maneuvers." The sale or purchase of various $100 million cement plants, which would fundamentally change the division's cost position and market share, were closely studied in Virginia and Paris. Joint ventures and alliances with other global competitors also were sought, as were radical one-time reorganization plans that would have spun off one or more subregional divisions. Because the decision makers were senior managers from outside the division, their knowledge of what was happening in the field was limited by the number of hierarchical layers and the lack of communication and information exchange between them. Because no big maneuvers were implemented, change remained elusive.

A Perpetual Transformation Approach

Under a new division president, a strategic plan for the southern division of Lafarge Corporation was rapidly put in place that was consistent with the complex, information-intensive, open, and unstable nature of the division's business. Strategy design involved active dialogue between cross-disciplinary groups of three or four top managers with the relevant people in the organization: sales staff, terminal managers, plant managers, and division headquarters. Front-line employees with customer contact and local operational responsibility were closely involved. During a period of several months, creative chaos was stirred up with the motto "consider all alternatives except the status quo." A number of long-awaited actions were implemented to instill credibility into the change program.

The southern division became more open and outward looking. New partners emerged, in part because of changing environmental legislation and public expectations. The division moved more decisively into recycling the by-products of other industries and became a more integrated building materials company. Ecological constraints and opportunities were addressed head on. Top managers spent as much as one third of their time on community, government, and industrial partner relations in this area. Distribution took on dramatically increased importance, and its function was reorganized to reflect this larger role. With the growth in complexity, there was a greater need to stay sharply focused. The division reasserted its long-term identity as a producer of a low-delivered-cost commodity, exited markets in which it could not be a natural player, and reallocated resources in sales and marketing to target priority customers in priority markets.

Division management took on a key role in interfacing with world headquarters because of the competitors, environmental positions, and technologies it shared with other divisions. On as many as five different levels within the organization, the system-within-a-system process of information measurement and control became more important. To achieve effective information management, questions of administration and measurement and control were addressed at the executive level rather than left to management information systems. By adding dimensions of asset utilization to measures of return on sales, the executive staff was able to instill responsibility for asset management into operations and to gain greater coherence with the evaluation by world headquarters of divisional profitability on the basis of return on net assets.

Results after Two Years

The process of improvement was not smooth. It did, however, yield dramatic changes in the bottom line. In the first year losses were cut in half. The second year brought a profit for the first time in more than ten years. Given the volatile U.S. economy during these two years, in which there was low or zero growth in the southern states, these results can hardly be attributed to external factors. If a rising tide lifts all boats, this change program was executed on the sandbanks.

Over a two-year period the division experienced a net profit improvement in the range of five to ten percent of sales. Where did these profit improvements come from? Although it is impossible to separate gains due to price level improvements from those due to restructuring or cost reduction, the following sources of profit amelioration can be identified:

- Elimination of unprofitable sales accounts
- Improvement in product quality
- Reduction in plant logistics costs
- Optimization of distribution (truck, rail, barge)
- Negotiation of truck and barge tariffs
- Closure of high-cost terminals
- Inventory reduction
- Improvement in accounts receivable management
- Improvement in handling in aging plants and terminals
- Introduction of new products
- Improvement in plant productivity

What is significant about this list is the absence of "big maneuvers" and the fact that each improvement itself represented a relatively small influence, often in the range of $250,000 to $750,000. The cumulative effect became significant by virtue of the number of actions taken.

The participation of large numbers of individuals and the visibility of direct and quantifiable actions had a direct effect on the identity and culture of the division. Employee morale turned around; customers and competitors understood the division's commitment to its markets; and nonperforming assets were clearly identified and improved or divested. Each manager had a plan to which he or she was committed, and the division as a whole invigorated its identity and acquired a positive vision.

Factors Underlying Successful Change

The success of the program in the southern division of Lafarge was due to a relatively limited number of key conditions. Changes in personnel were perhaps the most important—a new president and new executive council shared a vision of change, most line managers were given a second chance to be effective, and a few managers were let go because they did not want to change at all. The seven-member top management team that was formed in the process became central to the success of the program as facilitator and initiator of change rather than as "boss-bossing" decision makers. The executive council served the one thousand operating employees who were running operations, not the other way around. In this process, willingness to discard conventional ideas and ways of doing things became paramount.

A shared focus on delivered costs became effective only when employees began to understand that top management was serious about participatory management. Suddenly, the president was spending a large amount of time in informal meetings throughout the division. He shared his vision and asked what was going on in the minds of front-line employees ("the people who make our business happen"). He demanded better performance and listened generously to all ideas on how to achieve it. For the first time, front-line employees were given power to affect change; their opinions were solicited. As a member of the seven-person executive council, one of us (C.L.) spent most of his time in structured meetings with customers and working sessions with line managers. After the first few months of this, he began receiving telephone calls from sales staff from Amarillo, Texas, to Baton Rouge, Louisiana, to West Palm Beach, Florida, with ideas and suggestions that had an immediate and significant effect on the bottom line. Had the problem in the past been inertia or lack of responsible management? The problem more likely was that a coherent program of change had never reached the people in the best position to make change happen. In addition, a constant search for new products, new services, and new relationships with a growing number of players in the division's business to improve both competitiveness and the competitive dynamics of the industry began to yield results once a participatory and operations-driven program of change was underway.

A third factor in the transformation of the southern division at Lafarge was implementation of a goal-oriented information and measurement system. "If you can't measure it, you can't control it." Historically this division was mired in the past. From strategic plans to sales reports to financial tables, a mix of hard-to-use computer systems, traditional ways of doing things, and lack of direction produced hundreds of boxes of reports and printouts every month—a mountain of paper no one read or used. Existing reports hid unprofitable accounts, products, or activities. Sales staff resorted to volume targets, plant foremen to production targets, and distribution managers to throughput targets. The customer and the division's profit objectives were lost in the shuffle.

Under the new system, reports and printouts were few and were simple to use. They forced the measurement of performance in a way that conferred responsibility on the user. Sales reports took the focus away from volume and price and shifted it to net margins by product, terminal throughput, and territory. Terminal printouts linked inventory levels and product throughputs to net margins. Plant managers were given information about delivered cost competitiveness in the various markets.

The lack of design and dissemination of effective reports was symptomatic of a larger information and communication problem. Before the transformation process was undertaken, centralized staff functions (accounting, planning, management-information systems, and human resources) had been a closed system. Staff members wrote memos mainly to each other. Directives were issued to operations, and regular presentations were made only to top management. A large degree of insularity had led to one-way flows of information and fostered an attitude of "not my responsibility" and disconnection from the reality of front-line operations. Instead of facilitating the flow of information between operations and corporate management, middle-level managers had largely done the opposite.

The new conditions of operation and decision making became a motivating force in the southern division of Lafarge Corporation within six to nine months. They resulted in a profitability ethic that pervaded every activity. Although the gains achieved and projected were not sufficient to meet corporate profitability targets, and the division eventually reorganized and partially divested, the transformation program during these years represented a considerable achievement for everyone concerned.

A central theme running through this example is the forcing of turbulent change from *within* the organization. Top management has to produce the conditions for instability so that complete and fundamental change can reach new levels of competitiveness and profitability. It is only in this way that uncompetitive companies in down-markets can improve performance without waiting passively for the external environment to improve.

Chapter 3

Chaos Dynamics: Lessons from the New Sciences

Before turning to what principles and actions lie at the heart of perpetual transformation, we briefly outline the new-science foundation of this approach. Those in a hurry to get to the how-to may prefer to go straight to Chapter 4. Here the main features of evolution, chaos, and complexity theory are outlined and made relevant to the business world and its terminology.

The terms *chaos*, *complexity*, and *evolution* have grown increasingly popular in management circles, in part because they are powerful emerging scientific concepts. Yet their meaning is obscured by the common usage of the words. *Chaos* is usually taken to mean lacking order or without rules, and *complex* is taken to mean complicated. *Evolution* is thought to imply gradual change. In each case this popular usage no longer reflects the scientific meaning of the terms.

In the emerging scientific view, chaos has a subtle order of its own and can be understood as part of a distinct sequence of events. *Complexity* refers to the large number of elements in a system and to the intensity of their interrelationships. In this new view, a Boeing 767 is complicated but not complex or chaos prone. It has many parts, but the interrelationships between the parts are limited. The landing gear, for example, is not connected to the passenger video system.

Cause and effect are mostly predictable: you toggle switch A, and wing flap D is raised or lowered. By contrast, living systems (such as business organizations) belong to the class of complicated *and* complex, chaos-prone systems. The number of possible interrelationships within a complex system often is mind boggling. In the human brain, for example, connections between neurons number in the billions. The way in which neurons in the brain interact, the so-called firing sequence, is not fully predictable and subject to feedback cycles and fatigue thresholds.

Large companies fit relatively well the description of complex entities in unstable environments. They are complex by virtue of the sheer number of parts and the intensity and possible combinations of the parts. They are examples of complex adaptive *human* systems. Because people are involved, the degree of complexity is a quantum degree higher that in living systems in the natural world, say an ant colony. An element of choice about the future exists that is absent in other living systems.

These characteristics of large companies—a high degree of complexity and choice about the future—make insights from the new sciences of complexity, chaos, and evolution highly relevant to the challenge of leadership. Science has always been the primary knowledge base for understanding the world. Without science we resort to intuition, experience, luck, or religion. The natural sciences, particularly physics, biology, chemistry, and cosmology, have undergone fundamental change in the course of the twentieth century, and the change has consequences for our overall view of reality. With the change in scientific knowledge, an opportunity exists for managers to take on leadership practices grounded in more effective, up-to-date thinking.

MODELS OF LEADERSHIP DRAWN FROM SCIENCE

Business leaders operate with a default model of organization we call newtonian-cartesian. It is rational, logical, and reductionistic. The focus of the model is on reducing the organization to manageable units. The units may be individual persons, technologies, tasks, cost codes, or departments. In each case the idea is to optimize the pieces that make up the whole company—an exercise a little like polishing eggshell fragments before putting Humpty Dumpty together again. Leaders often assume that if everyone does his or her job, performs his or her tasks, and reduces his or her costs, the organization will somehow be successful and healthy at the level of the entire company. Also implicit in the newtonian-cartesian model of organization is the notion that change is predictable and incremental and tends toward stable states. This notion is rooted in the calculus with which Newton expressed his immutable laws of physics—smooth, continuous, differential equations that lead toward a fixed equilibrium.

In contrast, the leadership model that emerges from the sciences of complexity is related to organizations in terms of living systems. The focus is on the emergence of sophisticated behavior at the level of the organization itself. This system-level behavior cannot be reduced to the behavior of individual parts such as persons, tasks, costs, or departments. The leadership implied in the new-sciences model leverages the distributed intelligence of the entire organization. Knowledge is assumed to be distributed across a wide variety of persons and systems, and no individual leader is smart enough to control the organization from a central vantage point. Solutions require the alignment of many different opinions, interests, and constituencies.

The choice is not *either* a newtonian-cartesian perspective *or* a complex adaptive systems approach. The choice is to choose principles, rules, behaviors from both models, depending on the context. In implementing a product assembly system or writing a financial software program, the underlying newtonian-cartesian model is likely to be more appropriate: one wants predictable, linear, controllable outcomes. Situations exist, however, that call for solutions to emerge from deep inside the organization in ways that cannot be predicted or controlled. Technological leadership in terms of high rates of product innovation is a good example. Intended outcomes may be known, but the specific paths to achieve those outcomes are not. In these cases the collective intelligence of the organization—in sales, engineering, research and development procurement, and marketing—far outweighs the intelligence of the few individuals at the top.

Leadership based on the living-systems model of organization requires an understanding of how organizations evolve. The focus shifts from what *is* to what is *becoming*, from structure to dynamics. The underlying laws of change of such systems, whether in life forms or in the business world, are covered in the following section. The pattern of change in living systems is as follows:

- Innovation
- Complexification
- Convergence
- Bifurcation
- Chaos

The pattern of change in living systems can be grasped under the heading of a few key concepts. These concepts originate in the natural sciences but have business equivalents that we present in nontechnical detail for the industrial and corporate world. Because it is part of a sequence, each concept must be considered in relation to those that come before and after it.

Innovation

Innovation lies at the heart of all living systems. The kind of innovation that affects the corporation is primarily technological, directly or indirectly based on advances in science.

Such innovation is generally irreversible; the improved effectiveness or efficiency can be transcended by later innovations, but the impact cannot be forgotten. The irreversibility of technological change has held true throughout history, from the steam engine to the jet turbine, from the telephone to multimedia, and from the typewriter to voice-recognition software. It holds true today as we innovate fiber optics, genetic cloning, intelligent software, and electronic commerce. The main difference is the speed with which innovation is occurring. The impact of high innovation is made through the next feature: complexity and convergence.

Complexity and Convergence

Technological innovation injects additional flows of information into the environment, and these flows both require and make possible complexification of the corporation, industry, and society. There are, however, limits to complexity. If a system is to move within the limits, it cannot simply add more and more elements and interconnections to its existing structures. Complexity can be accommodated only through the creation of new levels of organization in which the newly created levels control and coordinate those that already exist. This means that whether it is a corporation, an industry, or a cluster of industries, a system always converges progressively toward more embracing and coordinated multilevel structures.

In the course of business history, convergence has brought together workshops, factories, merchants, firms, industries, markets, ecological systems, and societies into a more and more extensive, complex, and diversified system. The visible result of this process is the global corporation. The continuation of the process is bringing together corporations through various partnerships and alliances, including mergers and acquisitions, and bringing together industries through common standards and regulations.

What will be the consequences for companies that are already global players? Where will increased levels of complexity and convergence ultimately lead? No one knows the answer to these questions, yet the new science offers insight into the paths taken by all systems as they approach the limits of complexity and convergence. As instability sets in, the next link in the sequence is forged, and chaos itself becomes one of several possible outcomes.

Bifurcation and Chaos

As complex systems evolve, driven by innovation and converging with their environments into new levels of organization, their paths are seldom smooth and continuous. Theoretical scientists recognized this fact for decades, but it was only with the wider availability of high-speed computers in the last few years that the process could be understood with mathematical precision. The evolutionary paths are marked by so-called attractors that define the time sequence, the specific pattern, traced by the states of a system in an evolutionary trajectory.

The graphic pattern of such a trajectory can be visualized with the help of an imaginary computer program that plots system states as a sequence of pixels on a screen. The image made by the sequence is a visual representation of an attractor. Several varieties of attractors can be seen to exist. Stable-point attractors are characterized by a fixed point on the screen to which the system tends over time; periodic attractors are defined by cyclically recurring states; and strange or chaotic attractors model apparently random movement from which order emerges. In the case of chaotic attractors, the sequence of pixels on the screen moves from one seemingly unpredictable point to the next: pixel n in relation to $n - 1$ is no guide to where $n + 1$ will be. Yet a definite and often beautiful shape emerges from the growing density of pixels on the screen to show us the order inherent in chaos. Such visualization highlights a key feature of chaos systems: their evolution over time respects definite patterns and boundaries. They are not arbitrary and without order.

When a complex system shifts from one set of attractors to others, its trajectory forks off into a new pattern. The term *bifurcation* describes this pattern shift. Complex systems in the real world evolve from a particular initial state until a pattern emerges. If the pattern shows that the evolution of the system comes to a rest, the process is governed by static attractors. If the pattern consists of a cycle with definite periodicity, the evolution of the system is under the sway of periodic attractors. If the sequence of states neither comes to rest nor exhibits periodicity but becomes erratic, it is under the influence of strange or chaotic attractors.

Chaotic attractors are more widespread than were previously believed: erratic behavior has been found in a great variety of systems. The chaos models of the world's financial markets, the human nervous system, and the world's weather are examples. So is the perpetual transformation of large business organizations driven by technological innovation and other radical discontinuities in the competitive environments. So-called catastrophic bifurcations are especially relevant for companies undergoing an industry shakeout, restructuring, or an underlying technological revolution in products or services. The new sciences of complexity and chaos provide insight into how complex systems move from chaotic conditions to a newly ordered state through the reconfiguration of units, processes, and cultures. The chaos that intervenes in such transformations does not imply randomness or chaos in the everyday sense of the word. On closer analysis chaos as a scientific phenomenon turns out to have a complex and subtle order of its own.

The way in which systems handle complexity, instability, chaos, and a return to a dynamic stability is described by a natural science phenomenon known as *cross-catalytic cycles*. These cycles are the heart of the self-organizing process, which gives complex systems their unique capability to survive perturbations, grow, and prosper.

CROSS-CATALYTIC CYCLES AND SELF-ORGANIZATION IN COMPANIES

Consider the way in which any natural system stabilizes itself in a complex and unstable environment. The process of dynamic systems stability occurs through the basic evolutionary mechanism of cross-catalytic cycles. Cross-catalytic cycles are defined as the action and reaction of separate entities (in business these entities can be individuals, teams, departments, business units, or even companies) in such a way as to catalyze into existence a new, higher-level entity composed of the original entities and their interrelationships. A new system is born that has remarkable properties of stability and adaptability.

Cross-catalytic cycles are evident both *within* corporations and *between* a corporation and its environment. Within corporations, product development groups receive information from sales teams and financial managers and send out information about their work progress. The same is true of manufacturing teams, purchasing departments, business development managers, and so on. Each team defines the conditions in which other teams can perform their functions; one team acts as a catalyst for the functions of the others. Without the existence of cross-catalytic cycles within a firm, the processes of learning and of adaptation to external change would not be possible.

Between the corporation and its environment, we get what Michael Porter describes as a self-supporting industry cluster. One firm acts as a catalyst for other firms vertically through suppliers and distributors, horizontally through competitors, and, increasingly, diagonally through firms in related industries. The entire industry cluster has tight or organic properties. Any one player within the cluster depends on the welfare of the entire cluster for profitability and growth.

The evolutionary path followed by cross-catalytic cycles leads to convergence. Each cycle feeds on itself, develops itself, and converges toward a cycle on the next higher level of organization. Thus, loosely connected departments become integrated parts of divisions; divisions become subsystems of the corporation; the corporation becomes increasingly bound up in the health of the industry; and the health of the industry is inextricably linked to the natural cycles of the global economy.

RETHINKING THE GLOBAL CORPORATION

The rate of transformation in the technologies that underlie business activity, the globalization of the marketplace, and the rise of ecological and social systems stress have led to a quantum change in the nature of the business corporation. The power, span, scope, adaptability, responsibility, regulation, sophistication, and risks faced by present-day corporations are different from those associated with a typical firm a few decades ago. Thus, we need to rethink the existence of the corporation. With the conceptual framework of the new sciences, we can contrast the traditional concept of the firm to that of the complex global corporations of today.

The traditional multinational firm is largely a static, sum-of-parts, closed, and inward-looking entity. It is defined by activity structures, matrix organizations, corporate culture, shareholding structure, key technologies, and the quality and style of management. Its symbol is the hierarchical structure shown in Figure 3.1.

The complex global corporation of today has defining properties that are less focused on structure and internal resources and more focused on interfaces and the dynamics of change. It is a continuously self-organizing, open system capable of learning through interaction between employees and groups of employees and between them and the larger (and no longer strictly outside) world that extends beyond customers, competitors, suppliers, and other classic business partners to the ecological system and society. Figure 3.2 shows a new-science representation of a business organization in

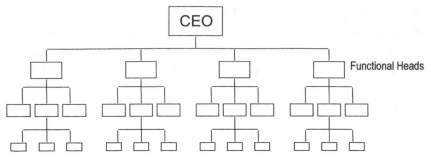

Figure 3.1 Newtonian-Cartesian Organizational Structure: Basic Command and Control

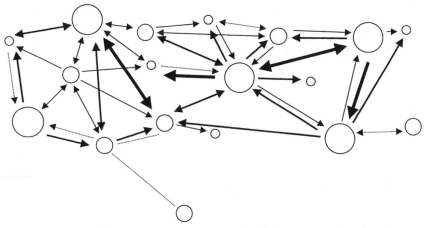

Figure 3.2 The New Organizational Chart: Network of Relationships

which the circles represent individuals, business units, or vendors organized in a larger network of relationships.

The hallmark of the system stage is openness to information flow. In addition to market, customer, technology, competitor, and other direct-business reports, the information base to which it now embraces information relative to consumer values, political stability, scientific breakthroughs, prospective government regulations, industry norms and standards, local community expectations, global ecological trends, and cross impacts with related industries. The amount and complexity of the raw data are staggering.

The principles of leadership in the following chapters are designed on the basis of the living-systems model symbolized in Figure 3.2. They stand in contrast to the default principles of management drawn implicitly from the newtonian-cartesian tradition of science. The essential features and values of the new science view are compared with the conventional view of the corporation in Box 3.1.

Box 3.1 Models of the Corporation

New-Sciences View	Conventional View
1. Company is defined by its ideas, business processes, relationships, and interfaces with partners.	1. Company is defined by its products, people, technology and hierarchical structure.
2. The future into which the organization lives is the source of change.	2. The past from which the organization came is the source of change.
3. Change is probabilistic and nonlinear and tends toward uncertain outcomes.	3. Change is regular, predictable, and tends toward stable points.
4. Company or division has irreducible qualities.	4. Company is the sum of its value-added activities.
5. Organization can be influenced but not controlled.	5. Organization is defined and controlled by senior managers.
6. Company is broadly integrated with its environment; everything is interconnected. Boundaries are fluid.	6. Boundaries separate people, activities, and units.

VALUES

7. Relationships require trust	7. Relationships require control
8. Many viewpoints, consideration of a variety of possibilities	8. Single viewpoint, one best way
9. Sharing, win/win, listening, dialogue	9. Right/wrong, win/lose, proving a point

Chapter 4

The Ten Principles

From global industry leaders to local mom-and-pop operations, companies are vulnerable to sudden and life-threatening change. This fact is not necessarily new, but the degree to which this vulnerability is felt *is* new. A few basic economic facts tell the tale. Growth in the markets of developed countries conceals the near disappearance of entire sectors, such as defense contracting and the emergence of radically new businesses, such as Internet merchandising. Many companies have been subject to the trauma of reengineering, which has provoked massive layoffs without improving financial performance for more than half of them. The rate of corporate failures in recent times is stunning. By 1985, thirty years after the Fortune 500 was first established, two hundred thirty-eight of the firms on the initial list had disappeared as independent entities, an average of eight per year. Since then, an equal number of firms have disappeared from the list at a rate of twenty per year.

The emerging context of complexity and instability necessitates new management approaches. Our contribution to this effort is aimed at reducing the sense of vulnerability felt by managers and at providing a framework for piloting change in ways that lead to constant renewal and a capability to survive frequent and radical discontinuities in the operating environment.

THE TEN PRINCIPLES AS CONCRETE GUIDELINES TO ACTION

The Ten Principles are concrete guidelines to action. They offer an integrated approach to the main managerial processes of a company: strategy formulation, annual budgeting, investment appropriation requests, controlling, and project management. By focusing on the conditions for managing change in complex and unstable environments, the Ten Principles are used to go beyond the mainline approaches used by most companies today. Current strategy management remains by-and-large static and reductionistic, whether it focuses on optimal allocation of resources, on productivity improvement and competitive positioning, or on short-term increases in stock prices. Current process management approaches introduce a dynamic element, by focusing on work flows, cycle times, and organizational coordination. However, as management commentator Peter Keen said, "Most [process approaches] are based on the assumption that a business will improve simply by refocusing on the customers' needs and concerns those operations that were originally designed to match the company's own priorities and structures."[1] Traditional approaches tend to deal with incremental change, assumed strategy, existing organizational structures and culture, and cause-and-effect remedies (make change X and you will get result Y).

The approach taken with the Ten Principles can be compared with other process management approaches on the basis of the relative *depth* of change involved and the *rhythm* of change forced by the interplay of the company's viability and environment. Figure 4.1 shows the different combinations of depth and rhythm of change implicit in a range of management approaches that deal with change processes.

The *depth* of change needed at any moment in time ranges from small or localized actions to profound and all-encompassing transformations that involve corporate strat-

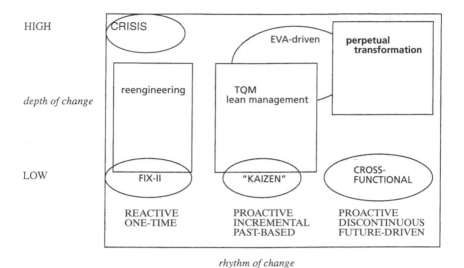

rhythm of change

Figure 4.1　Change Matrix: Approaches to Process Management

egy and organizational structure and culture. The *rhythm* of change can be reactive (typically one-time in nature) or proactive (typically ongoing in nature). Proactive change management can be either incremental and past based or discontinuous and future driven.

Here we have drawn together transformative practices emerging in leading global companies and shaped them in light of the knowledge base coming from the new sciences of complexity and chaos. The Ten Principles, although heavily grounded in observed experience, are derived from a theory of how living systems evolve over time. It is only by drawing on insights from recent developments in the natural sciences that we can find durable answers to many of the challenges currently facing managers.

The Ten Principles are not simple recipes or management tools. Economic value added is an example of a simple but powerful tool for determining whether shareholders are enriched or impoverished by an activity or a contemplated investment. Staying close to one's customers, operational efficiency, and benchmarking overhead costs are examples of time-honored recipes for success. Although not focused on the process of managing change, these traditional formulas remain important and, in most cases, complementary to our approach.

SYNOPSIS OF THE TEN PRINCIPLES

The issues addressed with the Ten Principles embrace the classic concerns of corporate management in the areas of strategy, organization, and execution. However, an emphasis is placed on the *dynamics* involved. Strategy issues, for example, include the process of changing strategic positioning, that is, how business activities are chosen and modified within an industry or cluster of industries (principles I, II, and III). They also include the way in which those activities improve competitiveness over time (principles IV and V). Organizational issues deal with structures that are best adapted to learning and autostabilization and with processes that allow complex structures to reinvent themselves or survive discontinuities in the operating environments (principles VI, VII, and VIII). Other issues focus on the role of top managers in motivating people and on the conditions necessary to unleash the full commitment and creative potential of the organization (principles IX and X).

The intrinsic nature of complexity and instability—the environment for which the principles are designed—means that they cannot be applied mechanistically. It is not possible to select one principle and, by applying it to a given business situation, hope for a simple cause-and-effect outcome. Instead the principles must be taken together as different but inseparable facets of an overall approach. They represent first and foremost a mind-set in the sense of Winston Churchill's dictum that "only changes in mind-sets can extend the frontiers of the possible." As part of a mind-set the Ten Principles are an effective basis for action that leads to corporate renewal and development of the capability to survive frequent and radical discontinuities in the operating environment.

Box 4.1   The Ten Principles

I. Create adaptive strategies. Multiple future-based strategic trajectories are needed in a business unit or company when flexibility and fast reaction times are called for in the face of great uncertainty—when discontinuities with the past make prediction difficult if not impossible.

II. Maintain long-term identity while repositioning. In fast-changing industries managers are forced to reposition core activities on an ongoing basis while maintaining a constant and widely understood corporate identity.

III. Compete for industry sustainability. The sustainable advantage of a company is inextricably bound to the sustainable advantage of its industry. Win-win rather than the traditional win-lose strategies are called for.

IV. Use strategic inflection points. Strategic inflection points occur when a company is confronted by a change of revolutionary significance that affects the entire industry in which it operates. Managers can exploit such key events and in some cases create their own inflection points as a means to a performance breakthrough.

V. Link transformation to shareholder value creation. Shareholder value is the point of convergence in the perpetual transformation process. It provides a reference with which coherence can be maintained between strategy, finance, organization, and implementation. Growth is shown to be a key link between transformation and value creation.

Continued

VI. Develop ambitions greater than means. The process of stretching people and organizations beyond what they believe to be achievable is essential to developing a culture of lifelong learning and adaptation.

VII. Design decision-making systems for self-organization. In environments that combine fast change and complexity the most effective decision-making systems are those that allow individuals and teams throughout the organization to contribute to choices and outcomes. Key elements include the role of headquarters, information exchange, distributed centers of competence, and learning by doing.

VIII. Fluidify the organizational structure. Decentralized multilevel organizations follow flows of information without the rigidity of hierarchical or matrix organizations. Managers need guidelines to creating and working in such network structures.

IX. Use organizational instability to catalyze learning. A measure of organizational instability is conducive to company learning and adaptation. Growth and innovation occur at the edge of chaos.

X. Reenvision leading: from command and control to (r)evolutionary influence. New tasks of leadership in complex and unstable environments require access to organizational intelligence and the distributed exercise of power for improvement in performance. Power structures inside the company must be viewed in a different way.

Integrating the Ten Principles into a coherent whole will change each manager's approach to complexity and turbulence in a large organization. The principles offer a measure of reassurance and influence in the whitewater world of business as it has come to be played.

LEADING COMPANIES ALREADY OPERATING ON SOME OF THESE PRINCIPLES

A number of leading companies are implicitly using the Ten Principles, although possibly through force of circumstance, intuition, or luck rather than any well thought out approach. Companies such as Lucent Technologies since 1996, Ford since 1994, IBM in networked-computing and computer services since 1993, Lafarge in the cement market in North America since 1992, Oracle since 1990, and Intel since the early 1980s have managed profound transformations of their organizations in difficult environments. The change program frequently is driven by a visionary leader with a strong intuitive understanding of transformative processes—leaders such as Rich McGinn and Herb Vinnicombe at Lucent, Lou Gerstner at IBM, Bertrand Collomb at Lafarge, Larry Ellison at Oracle, or Andrew Grove at Intel.

As Daniel Isenberg observed in a *Harvard Business Review* classic, top managers think in ways that are highly intuitive and integrated with action. "Since managers often 'know' what is right before they can analyze and explain it, they frequently act first and think later. Thinking is inextricably linked to action. . . . Managers develop thought about their companies and organizations not by analyzing a problematic situation and then acting, but by thinking and acting in close concert."[2] In the past, such a penchant for action worked well during periods of stable growth and known and knowable evolutions in operating environments. In highly complex and unstable environments, top managers can no longer rely exclusively on intuition and experience to succeed sustainably. The Ten Principles provide an articulated approach that managers can use to augment their natural abilities and past experience of what works and what does not.

Chapter 5

Principle I. Create Adaptive Strategies

Defining the future strategy of a company is one of the fundamental roles of top managers. At all times, the managers must be able to produce a synthesis of the information available to them and set the goals to which their organization strives with all its energy. Pursuing a single established strategic trajectory is no longer sufficient. No one is able to predict the future with certainty. Setting goals remains essential, but companies must augment their flexibility and reduce reaction times in response to unforeseen and discontinuous change. They must do this by visualizing alternative futures on the basis of probability-weighted trends. They must not narrowly define themselves in terms of particular structures, technologies, or products. Taking an entirely new path often requires selectively forgetting the past, sometimes precisely because of what succeeded then.

As long as markets, competition, technology, and other key variables evolve without fundamental changes in the rules of the game, companies can continue to strengthen their product offerings, reduce costs, innovate, improve customer service, and find other classic sources of competitive advantage. The objectives and stakes are widely understood by the organization, tomorrow bears some resemblance to today, and the anticipatory capacities of top management are sufficient to ensure continued growth and profitability. This is the domain of traditional strategy. It has come to include electronic database management, alliances based on information integration, supplier integration in upstream operations, and other sources of advantage based on time and information.

Traditional strategy ultimately relies on extending the past and present into the future. Benchmarking competitors, market segmentation, conjoint analysis of customer needs, experience curve analysis, and activity costing all are methods for improving future performance. They remain powerful tools for senior managers, and many companies have built their success and leadership with the help of such analyses and techniques. Progressive improvements in performance that build on the past and present remain an important element of future strategy. Examples such as AXA-UAP, Kellogg, and Toshiba bear witness to the power of incremental improvement strategies in surpassing or eliminating competitors.

Chief executive officers of global companies increasingly are confronted with totally new situations, which are proving to be unexpected and difficult if not impossible to predict. These situations arise outside all extrapolations of past trends. They represent discontinuities with the present and they frequently occur fast, snowball into a make-or-break issue for the company, and are complex to diagnose and use. Such discontinuities can happen at all levels of the value chain (purchasing, operations, administration, logistics, sales) and to all parties involved (suppliers, direct competitors, partners, distributors, customers). They necessitate a uniquely adaptive form of strategy management.

In an example from twenty years ago General Electric's competitive position in the U.S. market for refrigerator compressors was threatened by the arrival in 1979 and 1980 of

Japanese units priced at $32; GE's *cost* was still $48. Such a sudden competitive disadvantage for GE was not one to be overcome with incremental improvements. A breakthrough in cost reduction was needed if GE's product line was to survive. More recent examples of fundamental, discontinuous, and unpredictable change in a company's competitive situation have become widespread. Consider the following:

- Automobile parts suppliers to General Motors and later Volkswagen with the arrival of Jose Ignacio Lopez and his new rules of flexible and low-cost sourcing.
- The end of the Cold War and its impact on the U.S. market for defense contractors over a few brutal years. It is estimated that less than one fourth of the one hundred twenty thousand firms supplying the Department of Defense in 1980s still serve in that capacity. The others have shut down their defense lines of business or have dissolved altogether. The companies that survived laid off highly skilled and dedicated workers at an average rate of one every forty-five seconds for a number of years.[1]
- The opening up of East Europe and China in the 1990s, which in a number of industries increased the accessible world market by fifty percent.
- Iomega's Zip drive technology, which drove disc-drive leader SyQuest into the sidelines in three short years, and Oracle's overtaking of Sybase in database management systems over a similarly short period of time. Numerous similar examples exist in the field of information technology.

How should top management deal with such eventualities? How can strategy be formulated and implemented with a capability to adapt to the unpredictable? We suggest five key actions to implement principle I.

FIVE KEY ACTIONS

1. Create What-if Scenarios

What-if scenarios are not undertaken as an exercise in prediction; they are part of creating a mind-set that is open to radical change. If you are asking yourself what your company would do in case its future proves radically different from the past, it is probably already too late. Companies must integrate into their strategies a number of scenarios for radically alternative futures. Such envisioning of the future can remain fact based and issue driven, even if it represents a discontinuity with the past and present. Creating what-if scenarios is an important psychological factor in preparing an organization to make the best of sudden and unexpected change.

The syndrome of compiling quarterly reports and annual budgets can be extremely limiting to a company's ability to adapt to fundamental change. Although these short-term exercises are efficient and necessary for a host of reasons, they must not allow senior management to privilege the short term at the cost of sustainability by optimizing existing structures and processes in a world in which these structures and processes are becoming irrelevant.

Box 5.1   Royal Dutch/Shell

Forecasting to multiple horizons can reduce delays in response time by means of adaptation of the mind-sets of managers to sudden and radical change. Peter Schwartz illustrated this point in *The Art of the Long View*, (Doubleday, 1991). He described the scenario-based strategy exercises of Pierre Wack and others at Royal Dutch/Shell from 1968 to 1972. They produced two sets of future scenarios for the oil industry, each with its own set of projected price and volume figures. One scenario was based on conventional wisdom about stable and low oil prices. The other projected a price crisis and cartel production triggered by facts and issues known before 1971. The issues included gradual depletion of U.S. oil reserves, a steady increase in western demand for oil, and the growing strength of militant anti-west factions within the Organization of Petroleum Exporting Countries (OPEC). By exploring the full ramifications of this oil price shock scenario, Shell was prepared for the change. In the following years, it rose from one of the weaker seven-sisters oil companies to second position in sales and first in profit. By 1996 Shell was the single most profitable company in the world with profits of nearly $7 billion.

2. Define the Business Unit as an Evolving Portfolio of Skills

Business strategies often implicitly define the company or business unit in terms of products, structures, market segments, technology, or customer types. Such overly narrow strategic definition has inherent limitations in the face of sudden and radical external or internal change. It encourages managers to think about protecting existing revenue streams instead of creating new ones.

A business strategy based on an evolving portfolio of skills or core competencies can help a company respond more quickly to transformative change than a strategy based on established activities. In the face of discontinuous change, it focuses on "who am I?" rather than on "what am I?" Hamel and Prahalad give the example of Motorola's strategic mission in the fast-paced world of computers and communication: "Motorola sees itself as a leader in wireless communication, not just as a producer of paging devices and mobile phones. As a consequence, the company's charter permits it to explore markets as diverse as wireless local area computer networks and global positioning satellite receivers."[2]

Faced with the increased availability of cementitious slag and coal fly ash in its North American markets, Lafarge Corporation reassessed its strategic role as a supplier of cementitious materials rather than as a producer of cement. Slag and fly ash are by-products of other industries and can substitute for manufactured cement. Had it seen itself only as a cement producer, Lafarge would have defended against the advent of slag and fly ash as a threat to its core business. Instead it partnered with processing companies, steel mills, and power companies to integrate these by-products into its overall product offering. An evolving portfolio of a skills approach allows a business unit to adapt to its environment while remaining consistent to its strategic identity.

3. Use Information Integration to Build Flexibility and Reactivity into Every Activity

Computerized links are increasingly common between research and development and sales, factory, and design laboratory, supplier and producer, and producer and retailer. Such links allow immediate reactions to changes in consumer habits. Procter & Gamble is directly linked into Wal-Mart stores for its supply of disposable diapers. This link eliminates the time lag and inaccuracies associated with visits by P&G salesmen to Wal-Mart stores in quest of shelf-space information. Toyota's integration of suppliers along its automobile assembly line is another case in point. So is Benetton's system of color tinting its clothing line as a function of directly receiving sales data from member stores.

Better integration of information technology is only as effective as the organization that uses it. Front-line employees in sales, warehouse terminals, manufacturing, and research and development are very often the first to identify new trends in consumer habits and competitor offerings. They provide warning signals about small events that can propagate into large changes. In this context, we refer to chaos theory and the role of weak signals that amplify and overtake entire systems when complexity and instability are present. The sad fact is that in many complex organizations, top management is highly insulated from front-line employees. Middle management often acts as a filter and fails to communicate all relevant field information because of its internal preconceptions of future trends. Companies in which top managers are in frequent contact with front-line employees, in which decision making takes place at all levels with the necessary competence, and in which employees at all levels feel a responsibility and commitment to creating a common future are better at picking up weak signals than companies in which top management remains relatively isolated.

4. Create the Future from the Future

Global industry leaders increasingly create their own futures by taking the initiative to set commercial terms, to specify production standards and norms, to signal intentions to competitors, and more fundamentally to influence and educate consumers about what they will demand in the future. These initiatives allow companies to implement their own more profitable vision of the future instead of limiting themselves to existing rules of the game. A famous example is SONY's introduction of the Walkman and later the Discman at a time when neither consumers nor marketing experts could identify a real market for the product. When Renault designed its economy-level Twingo car, an initial market study showed that forty percent of the public hated its highly unusual styling, fifty percent were indifferent, and ten percent absolutely loved it. Would you have taken the risk to go against forty percent of the buying public? Renault did and focused on the ten percent who raved about the new model. By 1996 the Twingo had become the second-best selling car in France. If Larry Ellison, head of Oracle, had succeeded in acquiring Apple Computer and transforming it into an assembler of network terminal computers, he might have realized his own vision against Microsoft's' personal computer-based future. Such initiatives require vision, risk taking, and a willingness to commit the organization to a new order of results that may seem impossible given the past.

Box 5.2   Starbucks Coffee

Starbucks Coffee is positioned in retail coffee sales at the top end of the market. Before the arrival of Starbucks, the United States offered few alternatives for coffee lovers, unlike Europe, where street-corner cafés and a fine cup of coffee in the morning are a part of everyday life. The problem was in both taste and level of caffeine, the insipid American brew being incapable of satisfying Europeans. But wasn't the U.S. market simply a different reality? What chance would a single company have of changing consumer habits and tastes, in the process getting people to pay three of four times the usual price per cup? To succeed, the company would have to influence the future through its own creative leadership, which is exactly what happened.

Starbucks opened its own café-bars in a variety of retail locations. Libraries, stores, airports, and malls were targeted. Composed of a few tables and chairs, each café-bar was a veritable homage to the coffee experience. Coffee beans from the world over were sold along with brewing machines and accessories. The consumer no longer bought coffee, he or she bought arabica beans or a cappuccino. An American reality, at least for a specific consumer segment, was transformed in the process.

5. Selectively Forget Past Recipes for Success: Continually Question Assumptions about What Works and What Does Not

In traditional planning exercises, the weight of the past invariably conditions the methods and thinking applied to the future. The statistical quantification of past trends, the rigor of mathematical models, and the fact of including hard historical evidence in a structured framework remain important to the strategy-formulation process. But they also can stifle creativity and block insights about future trends. Second, prolonging past recipes for success can be a structural source of disadvantage in the future. For example, William C. Durant's configuration of the leading automobile producers of the day—Buick, Cadillac, Oldsmobile, and Oakland—into General Motors and the subsequent structure created under Alfred Sloan handicapped the company more than fifty years later. Under the weight of its nineteen individual platforms and a large bureaucracy, GM lost both market share and profit to more nimble Japanese competitors able to produce multiple models from a single platform. IBM's success in mainframe computers and proprietary software led to a similar handicap in the early 1980s. The world was turning to personal computers with MS-DOS application software, but IBM continued to bet on its past products and technology.

Forgetting the past is easier said than done. Strategic planners and production engineers imagine that they are always approaching the future with an open mind. They would rarely admit to taking any approach other than an even-handed evaluation of all options—whether the issue is product development, a potential acquisition, downsizing the organization, or a new information technology system. In practice, however, future options are colored by what we know of the past. Achieving a future-oriented plan of attack requires confronting our assumptions and mental models of the present and focusing on objectives with a greater tolerance for novelty and dissent.

Box 5.3   IBM 1986–1996: Ten Years to Forget Its Past and Reshape a Future

IBM, one of the largest companies in the world and the leader in computers and information systems, historically built a quasimonopoly in its product markets, such as mainframe computers, and in its service to large-data users, such as insurance companies. Then came the personal computer, which IBM chose not to take seriously, preferring to concentrate on large-scale processors, with which it had an undisputed advantage. IBM remained too entrenched in its own past success to reshape its leadership in the emerging product and service segments, which smaller and more nimble competitors were busy creating.

Between 1986 and 1992, IBM's stock price was halved and halved again. John Ackers, its chief executive officer at the time, had organized the company into thirteen business units and was contemplating spinning off a number of them. Signs of decline were abundant, yet senior management was famously unable to do anything about it: the company known for keeping its employment levels constant during hard times was forced to reduce its labor force from four hundred six thousand in 1986 to two hundred nineteen thousand in 1994. Meanwhile it incurred more than $20 billion in charges relating to restructuring, and its debt-to-equity ratio exploded.

Lou Gerstner was brought on board as chief executive officer in March 1993. He had considerable experience in restructuring large companies, experience acquired at McKinsey, American Express, and RJR Nabisco. While IBM executive committees were still debating technology, Gerstner asked a simple question, "What do we bring to our clients?" His approach was straightforward in principle: reduce fixed costs, listen to customers, and reshape IBM's portfolio of activities. Services grew from thirteen percent to twenty-one percent of sales today, and the mainframe activity was reoriented.

IBM took another unprecedented step. It acquired the software company Lotus, for $ 3.5 billion, primarily based on the future potential of Lotus Notes. Other major changes included a relocation of headquarters, a less formal dress code, and a new mind-set and culture. Today IBM is in the process of making up lost ground. Its sales grew from $62 billion in 1993 to $82 billion in 1998, its net profits are over $6 billion, and its share price has returned to precrisis levels.

Box 5.4 The Five Actions That Lead to Implementing Principle I: Create Adaptive Strategies

1. Create what-if scenarios.
2. Define the business unit as an evolving portfolio of skills.
3. Use information integration to build flexibility and reactivity into every activity.
4. Create the future from the future.
5. Selectively forget past recipes for success: continually question assumptions about what works and what does not.

Chapter 6

Principle II. Maintain Long-term Identity while Repositioning

Companies are increasingly faced with a paradox related to their strategic positioning. By *strategic positioning*, we mean the choice of businesses pursued, the geographic markets served, and the selection of activities outsourced. On the one hand, competitive advantage only accrues to companies that are able to *reposition* their activities on a continual basis. Shifts in the external competitive environment, such as break-through technological innovation, powerful new competitors, or stricter government legislation, can marginalize an exist-ing business or create new profit opportunities. On the other hand, sustainable management requires the establishment of a long-term corporate identity for customers, employees, competitors, and financial analysts in ways that are recogniz-able and translate into price, volume, or stock-valuation pre-miums. The paradox is the need to create and maintain a widely understood identity while transforming underlying business activities, including those at the core of the business itself.

CONTINUAL REPOSITIONING

Companies are continually adjusting their strategic position-ing in view of the changing realities of their industry sector. The objective of this repositioning is to capture the highest

55

proportion of profit margin accruing to the industry as a whole. The factors that determine industry profit allocation traditionally include bargaining power, technology control, and locus of value added for the customer. In many industries, these factors change continually such that many companies are redefining their activities on a regular basis. For example, insurance companies now subcontract data processing (their traditional activity) and are entering fields such as medical service provision through health maintenance organizations, automobile repair service through automobile maintenance organizations, and personal services consulting. Computer manufacturers such as NEC are subcontracting most of their parts manufacturing but are entering the fields of telecommunication and banking services. Cement companies such as Lafarge Corporation in the United States are entering the waste management field through waste-derived fuels, recycling by-products from coal combustion and steel mills, and solidifying the waste of others with special cements. In each case, the move into a new activity is motivated by profit opportunity to reduce costs, improve pricing, enter related markets with higher margins, or exit an existing business that is no longer attractive.

The geographic scope of a company can change dramatically over short periods of time, leading to transformation in corporate culture, style, and decision-making systems. When Lafarge, a one hundred sixty year old, $6 billion building materials company with an essentially French-American presence as late as 1988, invests more than $2 billion in emerging markets (China, Brazil, eastern Europe, Russia) in the space of nine years, are its cultural heritage and ways of doing business at risk?

THE NEED FOR LONG-TERM IDENTITY

Companies undergoing repositioning need a sense of long-term identity. Although they cannot predict what tomorrow will look like, if they are to differentiate themselves from competitors, motivate their employees, and build lasting relationships with customers, to name only a few of the long-term stakeholders, companies must establish and communicate an identity vision. Lafarge seeks to be the world leader in construction materials in a way that brings comfort, security, and aesthetics to building structures. Oracle seeks to become the strategic partner of choice in information management for large companies. DHL is a company that unfailingly delivers letters and packages overnight and on time.

A closer look at these three companies reveals that each has maintained its recognizable identity over periods in which its core business has undergone basic transformation. Lafarge's explicit commitment to being a world leader in construction materials has not varied since the 1960s, but its positioning within the global construction materials industry has changed considerably. It has divested its engineering (1970), refractory products (1981), and bathroom ceramics (1991) segments and entered the building paints, mortars, admixtures, and specialty products segments (since 1986). In the United States and Canada, Lafarge entered waste management through its Systech subsidiary and cementitious by-products of other industries. Since 1988, Lafarge has gone from being essentially French-American to being a truly global company with operating units in more than forty-five countries. In 1998, Lafarge acquired Redland PLC, which allowed it to become the world's leading producer of roofing products and aggregates. Throughout this repositioning process, Lafarge has maintained a core identity for its customers, employees, competitors, and financial analysts. Oracle's move into networked computing and knowledge consulting, and DHL's acquisition of its own air-carrier system are other dramatic transformations in the core business activities pursued by the companies.

Box 6.1   Singapore

The history of modern Singapore begins in 1826 with England's annexation of the country as a colony. During most of the following century and a half, Singapore developed slowly, primarily on the basis of its maritime commerce. Racially diverse with large populations of Malay, Chinese, and Indian peoples, the country suffered the invasion of the Japanese army during the Second World War before achieving independence in 1965. At that time, the economic situation was dire: thirty percent unemployment, social unrest, a large English military base providing fifteen percent of the country's gross national product and more than forty thousand jobs.

Lee Kuan Yew, the first head of state of the newly independent country, did not believe successful development could be based on the existing economy, which was largely made up of trading and small, family-run shops. He slowly began to form an identity vision for Singapore that was based on manufacturing at a time when the country had no industrial competence, no infrastructure, and few if any investors willing to commit themselves to such an adventure.

Lee Kuan Yew was determined to attract foreign investment. The competition would be stiff. Other, more advanced countries in Asia offered seemingly incomparable advantages over Singapore. Labor costs were low, but this would not prove sufficient. Lee Kuan Yew decided to make infrastructure development his first priority. A new airport, new roads, and new telephone networks were financed out of existing income, whereas other countries sought to finance their development with external debt. As things progressed, Lee Kuan Yew built the next edifice of his development program—social cohesion. To transform Singapore into a country more like Switzerland than a developing nation, he made a priority of crime control, urban cleanliness, and support for the poorest segments of the population.

Today, Singapore is the Asian tiger we know. The country enjoys full employment, even with a recently imposed minimum wage policy. The port city is ready to take market share away from Hong Kong. In 1995, industrial investments reached 6.8 billion Singaporian dollars, an eighteen percent increase over the previous year, in sectors such as petrochemicals and electronics. Manufacturing continues to be the motor of the economy more than thirty years after the Singapore's dramatic transformation began.

How should leaders reposition the very core of their business activity while maintaining a long-term compass that is widely understood by all? The following four key actions lie at the heart of principle II.

FOUR KEY ACTIONS

1. Maintain an Overriding Ambition

An overriding ambition is one that defines the essential identity the company wishes to achieve. Usually it is simple and powerful, such as British Airway's goal to be the world's favorite airline, Coke's intention to put its product in the hand of every human being on earth (Coke is now the world's second most available drink after water), or Singapore's search for manufacturing leadership. It is the job of the chief executive officer to ensure that the entire organization becomes infused with this ambition and that this identity vision is communicated externally as well. The greater the complexity and instability of the industry in which a company operates, the broader the ambition must be. Thus, Oracle's origin as a database software company belied its rapid transformation into information management and network computing. The company needed a broad identity vision of strategic partnership for corporate customers in the information-management area.

2. Hold Constant the Identity Value Added for Customers

It is increasingly necessary for companies to separate what customers value most in them from the choice of underlying business activities pursued. For example, DHL's customers value on-time delivery overnight. That DHL should buy its own fleet of aircraft or operate through regional hubs is irrelevant to customers, although these new activities represent a fundamentally new positioning for the company. MacDonalds is known for its hamburgers and french fries in a clean and friendly environment; expertise in foods procurement or training of low-skilled, high-turnover workers is irrelevant to the company's identity image with customers. Volvo automobiles have evolved from economy range to near luxury and from low horsepower and understyled to the latest performance generation of V70 and V80 models; however, Volvo also has managed to maintain its identity image as producing safety-first, family cars with understated status value. Everyone from customers and partners to financial analysts needs to associate a recognizable identity with the company's name, even if underlying transformations take place in underlying activities that the company chooses to pursue.

3. Reposition Business Activities to Capture Defensible Profit

As substantial changes occur in the external competitive environment of a company, the past basis for profit and competitive advantage is eroded, and new opportunities arise on the basis of a different set of activities. Only companies able to adapt will survive, let alone grow and prosper. The global corporate graveyard is filled with companies that could not reposition effectively.

Positioning decisions must always be made within the context of the total industry system. Correct choices depend directly on the competencies of others, the number of competitors in each activity group and their bargaining power, the technology available, and the location of the value added for the final customer. When the maritime transport of bulk cement became an economic reality in the 1970s, cement companies in France suddenly found themselves under attack in coastal markets from low-cost cement plants in Greece among others. By repositioning downstream into cement-consuming businesses such as production of ready-mix concrete, these companies were able to fight aggressively the imports and defend their margins at home. The source of change in the external environment can be diverse. Such sources include a new predatory competitor, such as Wal-Mart for K-Mart and Sears, a technological breakthrough, new legislation, changes in consumer values, and any other reconfiguration of an industry's basis for competitive advantage. Companies either reposition to survive or stay the same at their own peril.

4. Increase Use of Forward-looking Strategic Tools

Companies the world over have reduced their reliance on classic strategic planning tools, such as econometric forecasting of microeconomic trends, experience curve extrapolations, and other statistical methods. The external environment is simply too volatile, and too many discontinuities arise to make understanding of the past irrelevant if not a handicap in preparing for the future. Companies are increasingly turning to principles of management such as those articulated in this book—principles that emphasize a capability for transformation and that can give rise to the conditions for learning and adaptation that complexity and instability necessitate.

Too often, however, companies simply reduce their forecasting efforts, shorten their time horizon (strategic plans used to be ten years, then seven or five years; now some companies have three-year strategic plans), or operate primarily on opportunity and intuition. In many cases, these companies are beginning to realize that such *ad hoc* management is no longer enough. A new approach is needed to reposition a company within a coherent long-term framework. New strategic tools include better monitoring of trends in the external environment, regular reevaluation of the broader industry configuration to see where margins are highest (to see which players are making the most money), scenario planning, pattern recognition, improved ability to pick up weak signals in the environment, and rapid and coordinated decision making.

The mind-set for use of the new strategic tools is creating the future from the future. What counts is less the company's past (its traditions, market positioning, and competitive key success factors), although these continue to inform decisions about the future, than the company's strategic intent for a highly desirable future. The application of strategy becomes an act of creativity and invention rather than analysis.

Box 6.2 The Four Actions That Lead to Implementing Principle II: Maintain Long-term Identity while Repositioning

---

1. Maintain an overriding ambition.
2. Hold constant the identity value added for customers.
3. Reposition business activities to capture defensible profit.
4. Increase use of forward-looking strategic tools.

Chapter 7

Principle III. Compete for Industry Sustainability

In today's global economy, the sustainable advantage of a corporation is inextricably bound to the sustainable advantage of its industry. To assure long-term viability, a company must contribute to the sustainability of its industry, including suppliers, distributors, subcontractors, and direct and indirect competitors. This means competing on a win-win model instead of the traditional win-lose model. It also means self-regulating industry practices rather than waiting for government intervention. The result of competing for industry sustainability is measured in higher profits for the entire industry.

If this sounds idealistic, consider the ways companies competed in the following industries in the 1990s: telecommunication, defense contracting, commercial airlines, cement, petrochemicals, and multimedia software. These industries were as cutthroat as any, yet the individual players came to recognize the value of setting viable industry standards, coordinating technology development, establishing codes of behavior, and developing alliances and partnerships that contribute to the success of the individual companies and to the industry as a whole. By comparison, the commercial airlines industry in the 1980s and the computer hardware industry in the early 1990s illustrate the danger of competing for short-term gain at any cost without regard for the viability of the industry as a whole. In both these industries, total profit returns were negative for extended periods, and bankruptcy was widespread.

Competition for sustainability is not merely conventional risk sharing, and it is not limited to intraindustry partnerships. It includes a variety of linkages to produce new and sustainable profit opportunities. It can involve local communities, other industries, and public institutions. Sustainable competition also means self-imposed codes of behavior and industry standards as they relate to the exercise of power. Lafarge, together with two or three other leading cement companies, has developed a host of unwritten rules regarding pollution emissions, fuel efficiency, product performance, and community relations. When we compare the western and Asian cement industries with what existed in the former Soviet system, it becomes immediately clear what efforts have been made to raise the level of the overall performance of the industry. In the former Soviet Union, cement was a highly polluting and energy inefficient activity with variable product quality. The result was buildings and an infrastructure that eroded or collapsed over time and a very poor image of the local cement industry.

The future of a corporation is increasingly bound to the future of its broader social and natural environment. It is only through shared responsibilities and pooled resources that the enterprise and its environment together can sustain profitable development.

Strategic partnerships are already a reality in many spheres of business activity, and they are evolving at an increasing pace. In the 1950s and 1960s joint ventures were more or less forced on companies by political exigencies. In the 1970s and 1980s mergers and acquisitions became perhaps the most common path to growth. In the 1980s and 1990s, more varied forms of partnerships, including nonfinancial alliances, minority participation, specific-purpose partnerships, consortiums, and the like, became both popular and widespread. In some cases, companies could not afford to risk their corporate resources to launch a new product (e.g., the

Pratt & Whitney–Mitsubishi–Daimler–Rolls Royce alliance in large jet engines). In other cases, such as Monsanto in specialty chemicals, the requirements for nondestructive competition or the establishment of norms and standards with regard to the ecology prevailed.

Mutually beneficial partnerships are essential mechanisms of evolutionary management in a changing and turbulent environment. At least in the short or medium term, implementation of these principles is likely to call for some level of adjustment. Costs are not a useless sacrifice but represent a necessary investment in the future. Unscrupulous competitors, however, can and frequently do exploit the situation. Under the umbrella of industry leaders, it is frequently the smaller players who seek to lower their costs by avoiding the costs of sustainability, such as observation of production norms and standards, nondestructive competition, and low-performance products and services. This new manifestation of the free-rider problem is either managed through market forces, for example, by means of retaliatory actions or buyouts by industry leaders, or the industry as a whole suffers.

No corporation is an island, and none can develop optimally except in interaction with its environment. One competitive industry helps create others in a mutually reinforcing process, a process Michael Porter describes as the basic "diamond" of industry clustering. The diamond is made up of the strategy, structure, and rivalry of the firm on the one hand and of labor and capital conditions, demand conditions, and related and supporting industries on the other. The diamond creates the self-reinforcing hypercycle that lends industry clusters crucial competitive advantage. It explains why some industries are consistently more profitable than others.

Competing for industry sustainability enhances competitiveness rather than increases competition. Win-win behavior must be considered part of the functionality of business. Japanese management consultant Kenichi Ohmae[1] observed that the nature of complexity—economic, technological, and cultural—necessitates that businesses pool their resources and cooperate, even to be more effective in competition. Cooperation is doubly needed if ongoing competitiveness calls for adjustments that serve the short-term interests of one particular set of corporations and the enduring interest of the entire sector in which those corporations operate.

Sustainable competition also yields increasing benefits in the form of more qualified human resources, a nondegraded physical and living environment, improved long-term management of raw-material stock and other natural resources, and the avoidance of punitive government regulation and local community activism. Either the system as a whole evolves in a sustainable way or each actor within the system risks additional costs and possibly being driven out of existence.

THREE KEY ACTIONS

1. Extend Mutually Beneficial Partnerships with Competitors

Alliances may or may not involve equity participation. Their purpose can be varied; it typically includes risk sharing, setting industry norms, complementary competencies, new technology development, and cofinancing. Rather than regarding all competitors as enemies, consider at least some of them as potential allies. If you and your company are not building partnering relations with companies competing for the same piece of the pie, a key source of innovation and flexibility is being missed. Searching for these kinds of partnering opportunities requires win-win thinking, not cutthroat competition for market share.

2. Internalize Industry-level Costs and Opportunities

In pursuit of sustainable growth, companies have a clear choice: either internalize the costs and constraints that arise on the level of the industry or leave the problem to someone else. A problem left to someone else can lead to a government regulation, consumer outcry, negative publicity, and ultimately lower profitability. Internalizing industry-level costs and opportunities calls for strategic cash-flow projections that incorporate sources of revenue from price premiums associated with industry sustainability and the costs of government regulation and a degraded industry image.

3. Establish Codes of Corporate Behavior and Company Standards That Anticipate the Needs of the Industry Itself

Companies that focus exclusively on short-term actions and do so at the expense of their industry will eventually incur higher costs and lower financial performance. Although this has always been true, the response rate in a world of instant communication and greater public awareness is very much faster. Chemical companies that pollute, equipment manufacturers that practice sexual discrimination, clothing companies that pursue sweatshop employment policies, banks that embezzle all contribute to practices that degrade the expected performance of the entire industry. Conversely, when Monsanto pursues fertilizer products that are environmentally friendly, the entire agricultural chemicals industry benefits. What can appear to be additional costs of doing business in today's world can quickly yield better financial performance for the entire industry.

These three key actions are not only for the global industry leaders. All companies play a role in upholding minimum standards of business conduct. The yardstick is whether a company's actions can be sustained indefinitely without irremediable cost to the industry and its broader environment.

Box 7.1 The Three Actions That Lead to Implementing Principle III: Compete for Industry Sustainability

1. Extend mutually beneficial partnerships with competitors.
2. Internalize industry-level costs and opportunities.
3. Establish codes of corporate behavior and company standards that anticipate the needs of the industry itself.

Chapter 8

Principle IV. Use Strategic Inflection Points

A *strategic inflection point*, according to Andrew Grove, former chief executive officer of Intel Corporation, occurs when a company is confronted by an innovation of revolutionary significance (what he calls force 10x) that affects the entire industry in which it operates.[1] George S. Day, in the *Harvard Business Review*, used the term *seismic-shift syndrome* to describe events that cause players to adjust to fundamental changes in market rules.[2]

Companies are confronted every day with unforeseen events initiated by suppliers, clients, partners, competitors, and sometimes even distant actors such as research scientists or local governments. Every day, these companies are forced to react to such events, which Andrew Grove refers to as having a force of 1x. In general, at stake are incremental opportunities for improved growth and profit or a chance to limit damage. Examples of 1x events are familiar to all of us. They include the announcement by a competitor of a ten-percent reduction in prices, installation of additional production capacity by a supplier, a decrease in consumption of a product caused by unseasonably hot weather. The degree to which companies react to such events typically affects marginal performance.

Strategic inflection points are events of entirely different proportions. Companies must exploit, adapt, or fight such seismic shifts or risk disappearing. One of the underlying arguments of this book is that strategic inflection points occur with increasing frequency, and managers need to use them to their advantage rather than view them as threats to be avoided. Consider the situation of office information equipment manufacturers twenty-five years ago. Most were vertically integrated into machine parts with a core competence in precision tooling and parts servicing. The advent of the computer-based technology of the 1970s made all that obsolete. Leading companies at the time, such as Addressograph-Multigraph Corporation, failed to exploit or adapt to the new technologies and went out of business. More recently Dell, a recent comer to the personal computer industry, overtook IBM and Compaq with a unique direct-marketing strategy based on Web-enabled commerce. The end of the cold war represented a similar strategic inflection point for many U.S.-based defense contractors, and the opening up of China and eastern Europe expanded the world market by as much as thirty percent for many industries. A host of technological innovations, of which the Internet represents only the most flamboyant example, affect a broad range of industries with ever-greater frequency.

In the language of chaos dynamics, these strategic inflection points represent bifurcations in the life of a company. The resultant discontinuities, whether they involve adapting to a new technology, entering a new market segment, or restructuring the organization, will determine whether the company will survive in its new form or disappear altogether. The status quo is typically no longer an option.

How can managers use strategic inflection points to their advantage rather than viewing them only as threats? The question is asked relative to competitors because all the major players in an industry are affected by force 10x events. The challenge is to get your organization to deal with seismic shifts better than competitors do. The following five key actions are key to implementation.

Box 8.1

Example 1.

A senior executive vice president of Electricité de France, one of the largest multinational corporations in Europe, told us that he had spent his entire career trying to help his company avoid major breaks with its past. The guiding logic was smooth and continuous change. As he approached retirement, the executive considered that this might have been a substantial error. By avoiding break points, he had unwittingly contributed to deeper and more intractable problems linked to culture, folklore, and dwindling resources no longer appropriate to the company's changed external environment.

Example 2.

The president of a $250 million division of Lafarge Corporation in the United States purposely created a strategic inflection point by turning the organization upside down for a period of several months. After nearly a decade of losses, the division broke even the following year and made a profit during the following recession year. How this was accomplished is described in detail in Chapter 2. It is mentioned here because it provides an example of how managers can initiate strategic inflection points.

FIVE KEY ACTIONS

1. Recognize Potential Key Events and Act Early

With the fall of the iron curtain in the late 1980s, European companies were faced with new consumer markets and with a new manufacturing base for their consumer markets in the west. In many cases, the best opportunities for acquisition and greenfield investments were decided within a few years. Volkswagen acquired Skoda in the Czech Republic, Lafarge acquired one fourth of the Polish market for cement, Austrian banks pushed into Hungary, and French retailers entered Poland and Russia. In many cases the investments made between 1980 and 1990 redefined industry leadership. For example, Daewoo's acquisition of Polish car manufacturer FSO gave it a shot at becoming a leading player in western Europe.

Within companies local initiatives can quickly lead to transformation of the corporate culture. When one Wal-Mart store employed greeters to welcome customers in what was otherwise a relatively low-end warehouse environment, it became an instant system-wide success. Within a few years, the practice had been adopted at every store, and the company had built an image and style that contributed to its success far beyond the logistical cost advantages. The success of Nordstrom's with its customers are always right policy is another example along the same lines.

Managers often intuitively perceive the beginnings of imminent instability and change. A key to improving the ability of an organization to perceive weak signals, however, is without doubt the flow of communication between front-line employees and top management. Front-line employees— whether sales staff, warehouse managers, laboratory technicians, plant supervisors, customer service representatives, product developers, scientists, or purchasing agents— often are the first to sense changes in the competitive environment. Do top managers in your company know what is going on in the heads of these people? Are top managers chained to their desks writing memos to each other? These are risks for complex organizations in fast-changing environments. Efficient exchange of information between various parts of a company generates the ability recognize and act early on potential key events.

2. Approach Strategic Inflection Points as Opportunities for Development

Strategic inflection points often bring increased tension, risk, and uncertainty. Just as every cloud has a silver lining, periods of turbulence offer unusual opportunities for development that rarely exist in stable times. Recent history is full of such examples. Compaq, after starting in the personal computer market when this was still an expensive product for the average consumer, began in the greatest of secrecy to formulate plans for a more economical product. It attacked the market with an advertising budget completely disproportionate to what it had been spending in its base personal computer activity. Compaq's aggressive investment in a nascent market allowed the Texas-based producer quickly to become a world leader in personal computers and to produce them more profitably than many of competitors. Today, Internet-based products and services are creating strategic inflection points for a range of companies by eliminating physical and temporal barriers to transactions in a range of industries from banking to merchandising to education and research.

Box 8.2   Intel

Intel has successfully confronted a number of strategic inflection points. In each case, a near disaster was converted into an opportunity for vastly increased profit and growth. Intel began operation in 1968 in the field of semiconductors. This was at a time when it became technically feasible to increase the number of transistors on a silicon chip, which led to annual increases in performance and reductions in unit costs. This technological innovation created a strategic inflection point, which Intel exploited initially to produce memory chips for computers. At the beginning of the 1970s, Intel had achieved a quasimonopoly, which was quickly chal-

Continued

lenged by its main competitors at the time, Unisem, Advanced Memory Systems, and Mostek. Events quickly deteriorated. By the end of the 1970s, more than a dozen competitors had entered the field, and Japanese companies led the pack. To preserve market share, Intel was obliged to incur loses over several years. Finally, in 1985, chief executive officer Gordon Moore and his right-hand man, Andrew Grove, decided to abandon the product that had initially launched the company.

Intel reoriented itself toward microprocessors. As it was abandoning the memory chip business, microprocessors were still a relatively small and unstable industry. Intel managed a relatively smooth transformation. It shifted old plant capability on a distributed decision-making basis toward microprocessors, shut down units, and fired people when no other option existed. A decade later, Intel emerged as the leading supplier of microprocessors in the world.

A third strategic inflection point that Intel turned to its advantage began with its publicity campaign "Intel Inside." For the first time, a computer components supplier sought to create a separate identity directly with end users. Consumers were no longer buying an IBM, Compaq, or Dell product; they also were buying the specific computing performance of an Intel chip inside the computer. This publicity campaign proved highly successful. A 1994 survey showed that in some geographic markets, brand recognition for Intel was about the same as for Coca-Cola. The "Intel Inside" campaign also had potentially disastrous consequences when its Pentium product was launched in 1994 with a floating decimal error in quite unusual and complex calculations. Although the probability of coming across such an error was less than one in nine billion, a strong consumer backlash was directed at Intel Corporation itself. Used to dealing with a limited number of computer manufacturers and not with thousands of individual consumers,

Intel found itself overwhelmed by inquiries and complaints. The crisis was overcome only after the entire organization focused on consumer communication and recalled the first Pentium production lot. The total cost of the operation was $500 million, but Intel survived and emerged with greater customer loyalty.

For details of the Intel story, Andrew Grove's *Only the Paranoid Survive* (Doubleday Currency, New York, 1996) is an excellent account of how one company exploited strategic inflection points not once but multiple times to transform itself again and again into a global industry leader.

For every successful case, a larger number of failures exist. The main reason for failure in complex and fast-changing environments is an unwillingness to exploit strategic inflection points after the status quo is no longer viable.

3. Create Your Own Strategic Inflection Points when Radical Change Is Needed

Compared to uncontrolled changes triggered from the outside, internally generated periods of transitional chaos can provide an opportunity to initiate radical change. Managers can ignite a force 10x event if a continuation of the status quo appears nonviable, if certain conditions are respected. On the basis of direct experience with such efforts, we have identified the following seven key success factors:

- Produce a shared vision of the objectives to be achieved.
- Extensively communicate this vision internally and externally.
- Get people to consider all alternatives except remaining with the status quo.

- Adopt a bottom-up, team approach to implementing change during the period of transitional chaos.
- Change key personnel where entrenched resistance to change is met.
- Provide a clear set of metrics by which to measure progress.
- Limit the period of transitional chaos to the minimum time necessary to tear down the status quo and begin rebuilding a different future.

4. Increase Communication with and Dissemination of Information to All Parts of the Organization

Most of us are not comfortable during periods of turbulence and rapid change and end up spending valuable energy on anxieties about our personal situations. For this reason, at strategic inflection points it is important for senior managers to communicate direction and progress and to provide reassurance for the entire organization. People need to be listened to, and information must be provided at higher rates than during normal times.

It is surprising how often organizations appear secretive with their own employees. Senior managers all too often feel that information flow to the front line is a matter for the communication department through formal channels. They largely ignore upward information flow. In complex and fast-changing organizations, minor lapses in communication and information diffusion can turn into a major liability.

5. Avoid Disorder and Breakdown

Strategic inflection points and periods of creative turbulence are exploitable only up to a point. It is axiomatic among many chief executive officers that one must never put the integrity of the organization itself at risk. Therein lies a delicate balance: too little change can lead to stagnation and decline, too much can cause breakdown, loss of motivation, loss of quality, loss of people, and eventual decline.

Unforeseen strategic inflection points imposed from the outside (a new predatory competitor, a radically lower-cost production process, unbalanced government legislation) can be extremely difficult to control. The issue is not control in the classic sense. In complex, unstable systems, the issue is not deterministic outcomes but is probability-based influence. Complex organizations are remarkably resistant to stress and change. Even during periods when chaos rules, creative and productive change is possible. The example of Intel shows how a company can time and again rise from dire predicaments to rule the roost.

Box 8.3 The Five Actions That Lead to Implementing Principle IV: Use Strategic Inflection Points

1. Recognize potential key events and act early.
2. Approach strategic inflection points as opportunities for development.
3. Create your own strategic inflection points when radical change is needed.
4. Increase communication with and dissemination of information to all parts of the organization.
5. Avoid disorder and breakdown.

Chapter 9

Principle V. Link Transformation to Shareholder Value Creation

All living things evolve in ways that maximize their chances for survival as individual beings, as a species, and as part of the complex, delicate balance of nature. Survival is measured according to strict criteria of adaptability and fit with a sustainable environment. Companies are no different. The more complex and unstable they become, the more their evolution over time resembles that of living systems.

In the case of the business world, survival has increasingly come to be measured according to a single criterion: shareholder value. In a nutshell, the concept of shareholder value management is that the overriding objective of a company is to increase the capital of its investors. Because capital itself has a cost (usually taken to be the risk-adjusted interest rate), all investments that increase the value of capital by more than its cost are considered to be creating value. All investments that fail to yield a return above the cost of capital are considered to destroy shareholder value. Shareholder value management is the use of policy tools such as economic value added (EVA) to make resource allocation decisions. Shareholder value management is a powerful measure of financial planning and performance. Companies that introduce it at every level of the organization, from strategy, to operations, to new investments, to executive compensation, show dramatic improvement in their stock price valuation.

Perpetual transformation is subject to the same financial survival criteria as more traditional management approaches. It must create shareholder value or risk sanctions by the board of directors, loss of the confidence of investors, and ultimately takeover (internal or external) by a management capable of providing sufficient return on capital.

DIFFICULTIES OF IMPLEMENTING SHAREHOLDER VALUE MANAGEMENT

The problem is not with the concept of shareholder value as the primary yardstick of success. Nor is there a problem with the measure itself, which technically is relatively straightforward. The difficulty comes from the degree of complexity and uncertainty involved in today's competitive environment. The following three characteristics of complex and fast-changing competitive environments render shareholder value management a more difficult challenge than management in a conventional, stable environment.

- The value of a highly quantitative method such as discounted cash flow, which relies on numerical predictions of future earnings, is reduced considerably when a company faces unpredictable, discontinuous change. It is very difficult, for example, to build meaningful five- to ten-year pro forma cash flow statements in businesses in which sales three years from now are likely to come predominantly from a product or activity not yet invented.

- In complex businesses, detailed financial analyses of individual activities fail to capture the value added that occurs at the level of the whole. Two businesses with the same pricing and cost structures can generate the same cash flow at one point in time, but their future performance can vary dramatically with differences in their respective visions, decision-making systems, and learning capacities. During rapid transformation, change processes become more influential in determining financial performance than either structure or traditional processes.

• The larger environment of relations with business partners, local communities, regional economies, and ecological systems has an effect on a company's future cash flow. Although many companies have traditionally considered this effect to be so minor and so far off as to be nonexistent for shareholder value purposes, it is now becoming a factor to be reckoned with. This need to quantify the financial effect of interaction between a company and its larger environment adds to the difficulty of meaningful implementation.

The challenge of generating financial value added for investors will continue as long as the capitalist economy continues to exist. The practical problem for senior managers is to apply the new EVA tools in a meaningful way. *Simple* should not mean simplistic, and *short-term* should not mean bankrupt the year after next. The analytic and controlling approaches to carving up a business according to EVA has to be modified to integrate perpetual transformation rather than one-time (or periodic) shareholder value initiatives in managing a business portfolio.

THREE KEY ACTIONS

The following three key actions are intended to serve as concrete guidelines in applying shareholder value management to a complex and unpredictable competitive environment.

1. Create Probability-based Cash Flow Statements

Scenarios involving alternative futures have to be driven by exercises of vision. By vision we do not mean a general philosophy or set of goals, similar to what Alfred Sloan might have had for General Motors in the early part of the century. We mean building a picture of what the market and your company's position in that market might look like in the next five or ten years. It will probably not be a linear continuation of the past five or ten years. Prices, volumes, and costs will vary significantly according to different hypotheses relating to financial costs, competitor products and services, consumer values, and legislation. However, it is not necessary to vary all the variables that drive a cash flow statement. What is important is to select those likely to drive the transformation process and to quantify *their* impact.

Box 9.1 Probability-based Cash Flow Statements in Eastern Europe

Consider the opening up of markets in eastern Europe. By 1991 many industries faced fundamental transformations that could have evolved in any one of several different ways. Irrespective of macroeconomic growth, some industries modernized quickly and produced windfall profits for all players within a few years. Others, such as the banking sector in the Czech Republic, proved unable to achieve a stable and prosperous transition to the new system. In the construction materials industry in the Czech Republic, the following scenarios were built in 1993:

Scenario 1: Rapid Westernization

Main local producers consolidate, either by being bought out or through joint venture with a foreign partner; there is a trend toward construction techniques similar to the German model; European norms for product performance are adopted; multinational distributors and consumers of construction materials arrive. Prices should reach eighty percent of West German levels by 1998. Probability: fifty-five percent.

Scenario 2: Overcapacity and Cutthroat Competition

Both domestic and foreign competitors invest at any cost; a large number of players remain independent; consumers purchase on the basis of price only; national norms remain in place until after 2001. Prices reach fifty-five percent of West German levels by 1998, and the volumes of any individual foreign player remain limited. Probability: thirty percent.

Scenario 3: Continuation of Pre-1989 Industry Structure

The large conglomerates, or *kombinats*, continue to have a lion's share of the market while integrated into construction itself, engineering, road building, and related activities. Construction methods remain as before (heavy precast concrete, on-site production, low quality finish, labor-intensive application technologies); prices remain low, and foreign competitors are kept out by industry practice and consumer preference for domestic suppliers. Probability: fifteen percent.

Opposite each scenario, a different set of pro forma cash flows can be constructed for a proposed investment in the construction materials industry. With 20/20 hindsight, more weight should have been given to Scenario 2 (overcapacity and cutthroat competition), but the fact that it was considered at all in 1993 allowed greater flexibility in investment, planning, and operations as conditions deteriorated in the mid 1990s.

In probability-based cash flow scenarios, it is important to quantify as much as possible events that represent discontinuous change (for example, fifty percent lower cost competitor products, doubling of demand, harsh government norms, and intransigent local community opposition). Traditional analytic accounts based on existing cash flow variables can blind a manager to unforeseen developments. Sensitivity analysis and the exercise of scenario building itself are more important to preparing the organization for the unpredictable than is precision of the numbers themselves.

2. Maintain Explicit Coherence among Strategy, Finance, Organization, and Implementation

One of the challenges in linking transformation to shareholder value is to maintain sufficient coherence among strategy, finance, organization, and implementation in the face of unpredictable change. To the extent that shareholder value serves as the main criterion for performance evaluation, it must act as *the* point of convergence.

Consider the case of a company that had developed a profitable new business in a new geographic market. Success came about initially because headquarters articulated an effective strategy for market entry (acquisition of raw material reserves, network of low-cost plants, local partners, limited range of products). Implementation of that strategy succeeded largely because of a highly competent local sales and marketing team. Early results showed that after only three years, shareholder value was created by this new business, and the total return on investment was expected to far exceed the cost of capital.

Then incoherence developed. A new organization at headquarters refused to finance additional investment and required lengthy studies in each case. The best opportunities were lost. To make matters worse, a new expatriate was sent to be country manager. She did not understand the new business. Instead she favored another line of business better known to the company.

An unusual case? Not in our experience. The level of complexity in the transformation (in this case the development of a new business in a new country) gives rapid rise to points of resistance. Bottlenecks in the overall functioning of the company can sink the best-laid plans. The way to reduce the risk for such incoherence is always to refer to shareholder value creation. In the example given, if headquarters and the expatriate country manager had better understood the capability of the new business to create shareholder value, they might have given the local team more autonomy to continue its successful development.

3. Always Pursue Growth Strategies, Even When Downsizing or Restructuring

Strategies focused exclusively on downsizing, restructuring, and massive layoffs cannot help generate sustainable increases in shareholder value. Growth is not simply a financial lever of shareholder value; it is the primary source. A recent study of leading American companies analyzed their stock price performance as a function of strategies pursued during the 1990s. The investigators found that companies that had downsized over the period had market value increases of three percent on average; those following cost-reduction strategies had eleven percent average increases. Companies that followed growth strategies saw their market value increase six percent if growth came at the price of profit and fifteen percent on average if growth and profit rose together. Growth pays.

Downsizing, restructuring, and reengineering can provide a renewed healthy basis for growth and development. That is the entire point. In themselves, zero or negative growth strategies cannot durably increase shareholder value as much as high growth strategies. And high growth strategies focused on replication (more of the same) cannot increase shareholder value as much as high growth strategies focused on transformation. Growth always worsens shareholder value when a company is already earning below the cost of capital. That is why one-time restructuring or downsizing is warranted in some cases to provide a financially healthy basis for future growth. Our point here is that growth in the sense of innovation and learning lies at the heart of perpetual transformation. Perpetual transformation is a primary motor of shareholder value creation. This is true no matter what the macroeconomic conditions or industry perspective, as demonstrated by companies such as Lockheed Marietta in the highly recessionary defense industry after 1990.

In comparison with smaller more entrepreneurial firms, large multinational organizations often function in ways that inadvertently limit opportunities for growth. Senior managers in these complex organizations seek to avoid actions that could upset the existing rules of the market. They prefer to focus on reinforcing existing relations with key account customers, supplier partnerships, and core lines of business. Why change the balance of power when each senior manager has worked hard to build up control over his or her own little fiefdom?

The answer lies in shareholder value creation. In industries in which others transform the rules of the game, companies that do not innovate and learn will find themselves creating lower shareholder value. This will reduce their ability to raise funds and grow in the future, which reduces their value still further in a downward spiral of asset and share-price contraction.

Perpetual transformation and shareholder value are linked through the profit-generating capabilities of growth. Even if a company must go through phases in which zero or negative growth is called for, in the course of its life it will have to pursue qualitative, adaptive, learning-based growth if it is to prosper.

Box 9.2   The Three Actions That Lead to Implementing Principle V: Link Transformation to Shareholder Value Creation

1.   Create probability-based cash flow statements.
2.   Maintain explicit coherence among strategy, finance, organization, and implementation.
3.   Always pursue growth strategies, even when downsizing or restructuring.

Chapter 10

Principle VI. Develop Ambitions Greater than Means

Perpetual transformation involves a process of stretching people and organizations beyond what they believe to be achievable. By expecting extraordinary performance, you forge new perspectives on how things ought to be done (the what) and invent novel pathways to getting there (the how). When goals exceed the means available, most people eventually become involved in the creative and learning effort to close the gap between goals and means. The best people become self-appointed leaders of change, whereas most wait to see whether both the goals and the means are credible. A few reject the challenge outright. These change resistors typically make up a small percentage of an organization undertaking large-scale organizational change according to the principles and actions described in this book.

Companies pursuing perpetual transformation need to consider the following:

1. Companies that do not take on stretch goals will be surpassed by competitors that do. In the nanosecond marketplace of high technology, the future belongs to companies that continually achieve levels of performance unimaginable in view of their pasts. From the world of only reasonable businesses survive comes a new world of only the unreasonable survive.

2. The entire organization needs to be creative and innovative on an ongoing basis; there is little room for resistors or even passive bystanders.
3. It is better to find out sooner rather than later which individuals are going in the opposite direction from the change program.

Developing ambitions greater than means is essential to creating a learning culture that pulls together toward a common purpose. Because managers often cannot know what resources and methods they will use to achieve key targets five years from today, they need to invent the means to get there. Leading companies that have achieved extraordinary results frequently began their transformations when it was very unclear how their ambitions could ever be reached. The following are examples:

- Komatsu's call to overtake Caterpillar, the world leader in earthmoving equipment, at a time when Komatsu was a fledgling Japanese producer
- British Airways' rallying cry to become "The World's Favorite Airline" in the early 1990s, when it was widely recognized as being one of the worst
- Chrysler's ambition under Lee Iacocca to become the most profitable of the big three U.S. automobile producers, at a time when it was nearing bankruptcy
- Monsanto's ambition to become a leader in environmental solutions, even though as part of the chemicals industry it had historically been perceived as an environmental offender

In each case, senior management, often in the person of a strong and visionary chief executive officer, was able to instill an overriding ambition in the hearts and minds of people throughout the organization at a time when achieving such an ambition seemed impossible.

FOUR KEY ACTIONS

The following four key actions are part of developing credible ambitions that can stretch people and organizations in perpetual transformation.

1. Strive for a Future Not Possible Given Present Performance

Senior executives are accountable for setting a course that embodies a vision of the company and industry at a future point in time. This vision is expressed in the specific ambitions of the company, sometimes called its *strategic intent*. The ambitions of the company then become a pull for the activity of the organization, and people are allowed to act in an aligned way.

If a company strives for a future that represents a predictable and progressive continuation of the past, it is sure to be surpassed by companies (including start-ups) that seek performance levels that exist only in the entrepreneurial mind. The corporate environment no longer allows companies to set ambitions that merely extend existing levels of performance or to offer existing products and services in an unchanged manner. Industry is full of examples of competitors that break the mold. Product cycle times go from months to days, reliability rates triple, costs break through previously unheard of technological barriers. The only way for leading companies to participate in the future of their industries and to remain leaders is to find pathways to extraordinary ambitions.

2. Drive Top-down Ambitions from the Bottom Up

The more complex the company and its environment, the stronger the leaders have to be in setting and communicating overall direction. Because individuals in sprawling organizations rarely see the overall picture, the chief executive officer has a unique task to bring together key variables into a single, coherent, overarching ambition. At the same time, ambitions have to be lived and felt, not simply read and heard about. Ambitions that are handed down from above like edicts from medieval lords are unlikely to stimulate the kind of motivation, creativity, and learning needed in perpetual transformation. Ask warehouse terminal managers or sales staff how they would define being the best relative to what customers are asking for and relative to what competitors are offering. You will hear plenty of concrete ideas; a few may even be relevant to how to formulate the company's overall goals. More important, by listening to what people have to say, you will open up a heart and mind to stretching performance later on.

3. Develop a Simple and Recognizable Rallying Cry

In large and diversified companies, there often are many driving ambitions, frequently articulated at length in corporate mission statements. These ambitions can include market share leadership, a recognizable image as a leader in the field, a superior ability to innovate, responsible partnership with local communities, and superior financial performance, among others. During ongoing transformation, people and organizations naturally find it difficult at times to keep their bearings: a sense of reference often is lost. That is a primary reason why it is essential to distill the ambitions of a company into a slogan or watchword people can use as a compass in turbulent weather.

4. Choose the Right Time to Communicate Timeless Ambitions

Setting farsighted goals that involve radical change is unlikely to produce the desired results if the entire organization is still convinced that the status quo is perfectly all right. Individuals are not likely to learn totally new ways of doing things if they are not prepared to *un*learn what they currently do. Organizations often are best prepared to adopt stretch ambitions during periods of crisis, when the status quo has proved no longer viable. Organizations and people need to be softened up a little to accept a new set of ambitions that seem out of reach in the current context. We have found that developing such organizational receptivity can take years.

Unlike reengineering or downsizing efforts, perpetual transformation is not a one-time effort. The nature of such transformation makes single-event ambitions, such as cutting costs by ten percent, less effective. Because a company may look totally different in three years and again a few years later, goals have to have a timeless quality. They must continue to be valid after several transformations in the specific strategies and operations pursued. Companies that have adopted meaningful overarching ambitions with this timeless quality include British Airways, Ford ("Quality is Job 1"), Motorola ("Six Sigma Quality"), and Lafarge ("World Leader in Building Materials"). In each case, the company has undergone profound change in its quest for achieving its driving ambition. In each case the driving ambition remained valid over the course of the changes.

Box 10.1   The Four Actions that Lead to Implementing Principle VI: Develop Ambitions Greater than Means

---

1. Strive for a future not possible given present performance.
2. Drive top-down ambitions from the bottom up.
3. Develop a simple and recognizable rallying cry.
4. Choose the right time to communicate timeless ambitions.

Chapter 11

Principle VII. Design Decision-making Systems for Self-organization

Decision-making systems determine the ability of a company to execute its strategy. Without the capability to make decisions effectively, even the richest company with the finest strategy and best people is likely to be overtaken by more reactive and nimble competitors. Ineffective systems lead to a dangerous emergent core belief about leadership. Hardy and Schwartz described this belief as "This organization is run by incompetent decision makers. We can't trust them, because they will lead us to disaster."[1]

The faster the rate of external change, the greater is the risk that slow decision making will lead to competitive disadvantage. The greater the degree of complexity, the greater is the risk that centralized and top-down decision making will be ineffective.

In environments that combine fast change and complexity, the most effective decision-making systems are those that promote self-organization. These are decision-making systems that allow individuals and teams throughout the organization to contribute to choices and outcomes, that are open to information flows, and that maintain effective relations over time between headquarters, functional heads, and field operating units. They improve the following, among other things:

- The ability of the company to seize new opportunities
- The ability of the company to react to external threats
- The accuracy of the company's responses
- The flexibility of the organization and its adaptiveness to discontinuous change
- The adherence of the persons who will be charged with carrying out the decisions

Box 11.1 Risks Associated with Slow, Ineffective Decision Making in Fast-changing and Complex Environments

> Obsolescent products
> Secondary market positions
> Higher costs
> New competitors
> Unmotivated people
> Perception of weak leadership

In large organizations, people at all levels need to be involved in the creation of the company's future. If they are not and transformation occurs anyway, they will inevitably feel sidelined. One of the derivative insights from the new sciences is that the process of making decisions is as important as the decisions themselves in building ownership and commitment. People support what they create. A chief executive officer who makes all key decisions from his or her office is simply ineffective in the new view, no matter what brilliance he or she possesses.

Complex multicomponent systems, whether in business or in other domains such as biology, physics, or robotics, rarely function well on a centralized basis. Specialists in artificial intelligence used to think that the most efficient computers would be those with a single central processing unit. This expectation proved illusory. No single processing unit could meet the exigencies of even a reasonably complex environment compared with multiple parallel processing units with independent (but linked) algorithms. The IBM computer Deep Blue defeated Gary Kasparov in May 1997. This marked the first time that a machine "out-thought" a (human) world chess champion. Deep Blue was composed of two hundred eighty-six parallel processors. The Internet is another extraordinary example of a distributed decision-making system.

In the business world, centralization or decentralization is not the only dimension of effective decision making. Empowerment of people, vision, the ability to create excitement and commitment, and pragmatic issues such as incentive packages related to objectives all contribute to promoting self-organization. In the section that follows, we look at different types of decision making in large organizations that managers can shape accordingly.

TYPES OF DECISION MAKING

Decision making in complex organizations occurs in many different settings. Each provides top management with an opportunity to shape the style, symbols, and functioning of the organization. Are all decisions made in headquarters, including the proverbial choosing the color of the furniture in subsidiaries' offices? At the other extreme, is the operating staff left without clear guidelines as to how to proceed? Are the requirements in each decision-making exercise believed to be irrelevant or unclear?

Formal and Periodic Decision Making

Decisions are made in established frameworks and usually cover the most important management processes of a company. They include the following:

- Formulation of strategic plans
- Annual budget exercises
- Regular executive committee meetings

The participants typically are well identified beforehand, the expected output is widely understood, and the methods and formats are specified in advance.

Formal and Nonperiodic Decision Making

Decisions are made for specific events, usually nonrecurring, for which guidelines exist as to format, process, and methods. Such decisions include the following, among others:

- New investments
- Project progress meetings
- Downsizing or restructuring
- Crisis management

The participants are usually but not always known in advance. The expected output may be defined only in general terms.

Informal Decision Making

Decisions are made in impromptu meetings or casual conversations or are implied by what a perceived leader appears to favor. A good example was the case of a pending investment to reconstruct the administrative building of an East German subsidiary of Lafarge in 1990. The operating head of the subsidiary was asked by his team to approve plans for a new building. As he was leaving for Paris, the executive took the plans to study on his trip. In the hallways of the Paris headquarters of Lafarge, he ran into the vice-chairman of the company and took the opportunity to show him the plans. The vice-chairman's casual comment that it looked a bit Soviet style was taken to mean that the plan would not be approved, and the mystified East German team was given to understand that their investment proposal was not acceptable.

Styles and symbols used in decision making are powerful indicators from top management as to how much freedom, involvement, commitment, and adherence ultimately are expected from the rest of the organization. Styles and symbols that tend toward top-down, autocratic, hierarchical decision making reduce the benefits of self-organization. Styles and symbols that tend toward participatory, team-based, tolerant, distributed decision making augment these benefits. Henry Mintzberg[2] in his article *"Une journée dans la vie d'un dirigeant"* ("A Day in the Life of a CEO") described in detail a single workday in the life of Jacques Benz, chief executive officer of a large French multinational corporation. Mintzberg found that much of Mr. Benz's day was spent in listening mode with few direct interventions except to recall some of the company's basic values or to ensure that the long-term needs of customers are being kept in mind. How different is this picture from the desk-thumping boss of old.

ADAPTING DECISION-MAKING SYSTEMS OVER TIME

Although decision-making systems for self-organization present a general model for all complex companies in fast-changing environments, some changes in the life of a business favor one decision-making mode over another. The appropriate decision-making mode depends on the life phase of the company and its environment (Figure 11.1). The vertical axis is the degree to which the operating environment is new or existing. The bottom axis is the degree to which the company has technical competence and know-how in the business. The modes are as follows:

- If the company is operating a new business or is in a new market in which it has limited technical competence, it is in *pioneer mode*. The called-for decision-

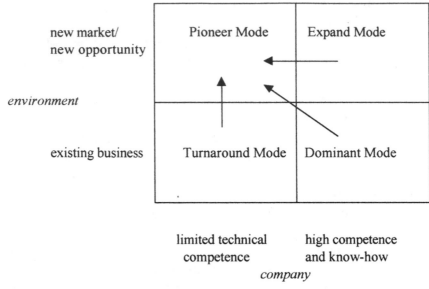

Figure 11.1 Decision-making Modes in the Life of a Company

making mode is entrepreneurial. It is close to the ground, intuitive, decentralized, risk taking, and informal. Entrepreneurial decision making in complex organizations can be assimilated to self-organization.

• If the company is operating an existing business or is in an established market in which it has a great deal of technical competence and know-how, it is in *dominant mode*. It tends to make decisions in an established and formal framework with centralized processes and a tendency toward global management of the business.

• The other two cases—*expand mode* and *turnaround mode*—usually involve a mix of centralized and decentralized, intuitive and rule-based, top-down and distributed decision making.

What is important in complex and turbulent environments is that the life-phase of companies is repeatedly drawn back to the pioneer mode (arrows in Figure 11.1). The constant but often discontinuous change in technologies, consumer values, markets, and competitors inevitably turns existing businesses into new markets and makes the technical competencies of the company a thing of the past.

Given that companies are increasingly drawn toward pioneer mode, no matter how established their markets and technical competencies, the main risk of ineffective decision-making systems comes from applying dominant-mode behavior. Unfortunately, in many large companies the dominant mode is the most common one.

FIVE KEY ACTIONS

How should top management foster self-organization? How can decision-making systems be designed to improve the ability of the company to execute its strategy? The five key actions are as follows.

1. Limit the Role of Headquarters in the Day-to-day Decision Making of the Operating Units

The best Fortune 500 companies operate with world headquarters of less than one hundred eighty persons. These people, including senior executive managers, represent the strategic nerve center of organizations that may encompass hundreds of business units and tens of thousands of employees. The decision-making roles of headquarters range from defining overall strategy to assisting in day-to-day operating decisions, although companies that promote self-organization limit the latter. The ideal distribution of functions performed by headquarters, compared with the situation in many companies today, is suggested in Box 11.2.

Box 11.2 Roles of World Headquarters

Role	Ideal Distribution (Self-organization Model)	Typical Distribution (Conventional Model)
Strategy formulation, methods definition, missions, policies, culture	50%	20%
Financial control and audit	30%	30%
Setting, coordinating, and approval of overall business units plans	10%	25%
Direct assistance with operations	10%	25%
Total	100%	100%

Efforts must be made to diagnose the real as opposed to perceived roles played by world headquarters. An overextended role is not a sign of better management; it is a block to effective self-organization of the business units, teams, and individuals who make up the company. The same is true of functional departments with multiunit responsibilities. The exact extent to which the role of a company or functional headquarters should be limited depends on the nature of the business and the degree to which the company possesses centralized technical competence and know-how. No matter what the case, self-organization favors a reduced directing role of headquarters.

2. Increase Informal Exchanges between Top Management and Employees Outside Hierarchical Reporting Lines

As complexity and rapid change increase, interactions between the components of a system grow in importance relative to their structure. How information flows between people, departments, project teams, and divisions becomes essential to self-organization. Knowledge, particularly knowledge distributed throughout the organization, depends on continual information exchange at all levels. The Internet is once again an excellent example of a living body of knowledge that does not depend on any central management. Instead information morphs through the multiple exchanges that occur across the Net.

To achieve effective information exchanges between top management and employees, these exchanges have to be the following:

- Informal. They are outside institutionalized management processes such as budgeting, financial reporting, and strategic planning.
- Outside hierarchical reporting lines. Exchanges that are issue driven or based on specific goals or projects are likely to be more substantive than exchanges driven by hierarchical reporting relationships.
- Deeply vertical. Exchanges should involve managers at least three levels apart. A division head should communicate with sales staff or purchasing agents not only their direct supervisors.
- Frequent. Visits by top managers less than once a quarter become largely formal and symbolic exercises and rarely allow frank and open exchanges.

3. Push Multicompetence Teams Close to Customers and to Front-line Operations

The need for cross-disciplinary teams has become increasingly apparent in recent times. The concept was popularized by Japanese firms that sent new managers through various functions and departments over the courses of their careers. Strategic plans written by a team of planners, products designed exclusively by marketing experts, and production lines run without customer feedback or financial control are some of the overspecialized approaches that have largely failed to take into account the high number of variables needed for adaptation and survival. All teams that deal with transformative change need to include a broad range of profiles, including at least the following:

- A regional or functional market manager with overall responsibility for the business
- Technical experts (engineers, designers, product specialists, scientists)
- A numbers cruncher (controlling and reporting)
- Functional managers (purchasing, logistics, marketing and sales, customer service)

These multicompetence teams need to stay close to customers and front-line operations no matter what the project or mission. A related concern is the widespread practice of appointing a project head distant from operations or the market. For example, large multinational corporations often give preference to managers who come from the head office, are of the same nationality as and speak the same language as the head office, and have financial or planning skills rather than local-market or hands-on experience.

Self-organization implies having many local centers of competence and leadership. Each center is focused in its particular area of operation. Such distributed decision-making power implies making the most of diversity. In this context, it is often useful to remember that the blue-suited managers at the head office are providing a service to the people who make the business work, not the other way around.

4. Be Willing to Learn by Doing

Learning by doing is called for especially when competencies and technical know-how are relatively limited (*pioneer mode*). Companies that face unexpected challenges in their operating environments tend to analyze, quantify, produce reports, convene meetings, and articulate comprehensive plans for how to act. The same is true when a person or team proposes a radically new and expensive investment project. When complex organizations are involved, the multiple layers and formal requirements for jumping through the hoops can lead to long lead times, distorted conclusions, and ineffective action. It is an inescapable law of the market that complex companies face at least one specialized competitor that can put ideas into action faster and more effectively by doing first and learning in the process.

Companies need to minimize risk through all the traditional decision-making procedures. At the same time they need to give project and field teams greater autonomy and trust to act before company or functional headquarters has fully assessed the consequences. In effect companies need to say, "We don't know everything necessary to carry out the proposed action, but once the key guidelines are followed, we will act and then learn as we go along."

5. Increase the Accountability of Operating Units and Improve the Link between Compensation and Performance Objectives

Self-organization implies the commitment of the entire organization, not only the chief executive officer. Yet how widespread is the practice of dissociating management compensation incentives from the performance of the company. In large numbers of multinational corporations, hundreds of operating managers receive only limited variable bonuses, often in the range of ten to twelve percent, which are largely dependent on purely individual target achievements. In the same companies the top ten or twenty executives can obtain cash bonus and stock options worth many multiples of their base salary.

Coherent decision-making systems that promote self-organization require that all decision makers share in the success and failure of value-creating operations. Today the financial instruments needed for associating employee compensation with business unit performance exist. They include economic value added analysis of performance by business unit, employee stock purchase plans, employer contributions to retirement accounts, cash bonuses, and stock options, among many others. Although a number of companies are expanding employee involvement, for example, most employees at Intel are company shareholders, the use of direct links between compensation and performance remains limited.

Companies such as Thermo Electron, the diversified energy and environmental equipment maker, are exceptions. Thermo Electron has pioneered the practice of spinouts, in which it hands over day-to-day control of newly formed subsidiaries and fistfuls of share options to the staff. This compensation system has led to the making of tens of millionaires among the more successful ventures. To encourage the managers of spin-outs to couple their strategies with that of the entire group, these share options are typically split so that forty percent are linked to the performance of the own spin-out, forty percent to that of Thermo Electron itself, and twenty percent to that of siblings. Since 1983, when founder and chairman George Hatsopoulos began using this practice into place, Thermo's compound return to shareholders has averaged twenty-eight percent a year.[3]

Box 11.3 The Five Actions that Lead to Implementing Principle VII: Design Decision-making Systems for Self-organization

1. Limit the role of headquarters in day-to-day decision making of the operating units.
2. Increase informal exchanges between top management and employees outside hierarchical reporting lines.
3. Push multicompetence teams close to customers and front-line operations.
4. Be willing to learn by doing.
5. Increase accountability of operating units and improve the link between compensation and performance objectives.

Chapter 12

Principle VIII. Fluidify the Organizational Structure

The structures that best support perpetual transformation are those designed to follow flows of information without the rigidity of centralized or matrix forms of organization. Corporations with complex structures and markets on a global scale need organizational structures that enable them to access, process, and act on information flexibly and efficiently. Functionally decentralized multilevel organizations are not hierarchical but what we call *community-based*. They provide considerable autonomy vertically and considerable coordination between horizontal units. They are networks of relationships. Information and task allocations flow diagonally through the organization. Such fluid structures adapt to fundamental changes in the operating environment.

Although he built his reputation after the Second World War as a management consultant to large multinational corporations such as General Motors, Peter Drucker no longer believes that the future belongs to traditional hierarchical structures: "The majority of my students no longer want to hear about giant organizations. And after having started their career in these multinationals, no doubt because of aggressive recruiting campaigns on campus, these young executives leave to join small and mid-sized companies where the level of personal reward is much higher." According to Drucker, the organizational structure of the future is the Chinese clan.

The Chinese are in the process of transforming their family organizations into multinational companies with fluid and adaptive structures. The only limit to success of the Chinese model, according to Drucker, is their capacity to integrate non-Chinese managers.

Complex, multipart systems rarely function well on a rigid, centralized basis. The specifics of each local activity necessitate an empowered field organization able to learn and act in accordance with global considerations. *How* decentralization is made to occur depends fundamentally on the conditions necessary for self-learning. These conditions depend on the natural information flows necessary to make rapid and relevant decisions. In some cases these conditions involve multidisciplinary task forces with a limited duration or service. In other cases, interfacing within the same function (e.g., within sales) allows otherwise isolated persons to compare experiences and approaches. In still other cases, strategic planners are made to facilitate and structure information flows between top management and the front line in iterative learning processes. Some activities, however, such as purchasing and research and development, provide economies of scale or experience that call for centralization. Even without economies of scale or experience, in some businesses pricing and credit policies are best handled on a centralized basis.

Centralization of operations in some areas within an organization is tempered increasingly with functional decentralization in others. The applicable model is not the human organism, a centralized entity governed by the autonomous higher nervous system (the most sophisticated system of management could not match the power of a system of ten billion neurons multiply connected in dynamical neural networks). The appropriate model is a problem-solving robot.

Workers in artificial intelligence used to think that the most efficient robots would be those with a single centralized learning-deciding capability to confront all eventualities. This expectation was illusory: no central-processor robot could be built that could meet the exigencies even of a reasonably complex environment. The sheer number of possibilities soon surpassed the computing power of even the most sophisticated central processor. To function successfully, however, several distinct information-processing centers in the robot needed only to be connected with each other and subjected to simple learning algorithms. Such a decentralized-learning robot could, for example, walk over more complex terrain for a longer time than any centralized-deciding robot.

When corporations reach a certain size and complexity, earlier structures based mainly on personal power and competence no longer work. At that point viable firms shift to a more organized matrix structure. As multiple interfaces increase, however, both within the enterprise, and between the enterprise and its relevant environment, the matrix structure also begins to prove inadequate. Most globally operating companies have learned this lesson: they—as did Asea Brown Boveri some years ago and Lafarge and General Motors more recently—transformed from top-heavy matrix organizations into flexibly coordinated network-like structures.

Multiple levels of decision-making capability bring multiple advantages. Catalytic cycles (see Chapter 3) can bring together the various levels and coordinate the functions of units, departments, and divisions to ensure that each contributes optimally to the goals of the entire corporation. Such cycles that coordinate multiple levels can optimize the use of limited resources, particularly human resources, by means of integrating allocation in view of system-wide needs. Multiple levels create the flexibility to engender localized change, without necessarily involving all the other levels above or below.

Managing a community-based system does not call for rigid control at the highest level. It calls for delegation toward the front line, coordination, and creation of ever-important conditions for self-learning at each level. Decisions can be made as closely as possible to the front line and rules established (for example, capital expenditures over a certain amount) for involving other levels. Executives thereby are spared the all-too-frequent temptation to become involved in micromanagement of each local office.

Strategies developed in community-based structures are a more effective and creative response to the demands of a changing business environment than are the best thought-out strategies excogitated at headquarters and enforced in vertically extended hierarchies. In community-based structures, executives are not required to specify the goals and means of achieving them at each level. The managers merely set an overall course one level toward the front line and create the conditions for subsequent levels to learn and make their own decisions in a cascading process of open-communication delegation.

Multinational corporations are typically organized along hierarchical lines of responsibility for geographic markets, product markets, or customer segments. These business unit organizations intersect with functional lines of responsibility where needed (marketing, research and development, strategy, controlling). A characteristic of these organizations is that structure is defined by the existence of general and repeatable activities, such as producing and selling a given range of products in a given geographic market. When discontinuities are introduced and an ongoing process of reinventing the company's business is at stake, these traditional structures have well-known limitations. Alternative solutions of flattening the organization through downsizing and restructuring efforts that eliminate much of the role of middle management have also proved to have limited value.

THREE KEY ACTIONS

The following three key actions serve to fluidify heavy hierarchical structures without eliminating key layers of management and without one-time restructuring. These actions represent ongoing efforts to give multinational organizations greater flexibility and adaptability in dealing with change.

1. Define Community-based Structures to Meet Specific Objectives

More fluid forms of organizational structure result from multilevel project-based management, in which hierarchical relationships are bypassed for a limited time to serve a specific objective. When multilevel project teams become a permanent feature of an organization, the organizational structure is community-based. It is decentralized and multilevel and driven by specific objectives that correspond to the needs of the business at a particular moment. Discontinuities are integrated into the organization through new structures that involve different people and new teams that fit the changed environment.

Senior management must define and communicate the specific objectives around which community-based structures form. These objectives can be financial (for example, a target return on net assets), market share related, cost related, customer satisfaction related, or process related (for example, to turn over new products at a given rate per five-year period). The metrics by which performance is measured must be clear and relate to both the individual entity (person or project team) and the company as a whole. However, the *organization* of people and resources around the specific objectives should be delegated to the lowest level possible. If the specific business objective is the result of a new development in the competitive environment, chances are that the existing organizational structure will not be the most efficient one possible. Chances are that senior management will not be best placed to decide alone on the most appropriate new structure.

2. Accept Lack of Clarity in Organizational Structures but Always Clearly Define Responsibility for Results

People always want to know who is their immediate boss and how many people report directly to them. In community-based organizations, such clarity is not always possible precisely because people are obliged to work together outside hierarchical reporting lines and around specific objectives. When perpetual transformation becomes a modus operandium of a company, the organizational structure itself undergoes permanent change. A technical manager may find himself or herself working at one level on a project in country A and then working on another level on a different project in country B. The extent of his or her decision-making power may vary considerably between the two cases and may not be obvious at the start.

This does not equate with anarchy (although it does create a necessary level of discomfort, see Chapter 13). The basic rules of operating with perpetual change include clearly defined objectives and clear responsibility for teams and projects. Corresponding to each specific objective as it is applied to a given situation there must be a recognized leader. If the objective is to develop new customer services around an existing product in a new geographic market, business developers, financial controllers, technical managers, and country managers may be involved. But one person in the group must have overall responsibility for the results.

Community-based systems with specific objectives and defined responsibility for results but with nonmandated organizational structures have the flexibility to learn and adapt according to need. This capacity is essential to what is meant by the term *self-organization*.

3. Facilitate Information Flow and Communication across Hierarchical Lines

Increased openness to information and communication corresponds to more complex and autonomous structures, from mass production to globalization and distributed decision making. Advances in information technology make more interconnections feasible (handheld computers, netmeetings, videoconferencing, direct data links), but the desire to use this technology is a matter of management will.

Community-based organizations depend heavily on information flows from outside hierarchical reporting lines. When discontinuities arise, and a new suborganization is called for, information from all parts of the organization contributes to efficient reconfiguration. The challenge is no longer accessing or transmitting information; it concerns more selection and relevance. Community-based structures depend to a great extent on information flow and communication across hierarchical lines for the process of self-learning and self-configuration.

Box 12.1 The Three Actions That Lead to Implementing Principle VIII: Fluidify the Organization Structure

---

1. Define community-based structures to meet specific objectives.
2. Accept lack of clarity in organizational structures but always define clearly responsibility for results.
3. Facilitate information flow and communication across hierarchical lines.

Chapter 13

Principle IX. Use Organizational Instability to Catalyze Learning

When everything is constantly changing in the marketplace, and the future no longer resembles the past, internal organizational cultures that overemphasize stability can limit creativity and learning. If news of a substitute product or major investment by a direct competitor provokes a series of meetings and a flurry of memos and a consensus on what to do that does not make anyone too uncomfortable, perhaps the forces of corporate stability are stronger than they should be. The same is true when members of a company's executive committee become more interested in maintaining personal agendas than in the future needs of the organization.

Past-driven, don't-rock-the-boat management styles developed in times of steady and predictable growth can hurt the ability of an organization to handle rapid and discontinuous change. Conversely, organizational cultures that succeed in institutionalizing instability can be factors for adaptation and learning. Institutionalized instability can work, however, only if it does not become excessive and only if it is balanced by process controls and counterbalancing benefits.

HOW WE TRY TO AVOID TENSION AND INSTABILITY IN OUR JOBS

As managers inside large organizations, we have long been told that performance is measured on the basis of achievement of quantifiable objectives, whether they be stock price increases for a chief executive officer, making the annual budget for a line manager, customer satisfaction, cost reductions, or service improvements. In striving for new levels of performance, we search for stability and predictability. Stylistically we do it in ways that promote harmony with our colleagues, that limit personnel turnover, and that give us the peace of mind of a job well done. We have become used to a step-function progression of setting goals and striving to reach them then setting new goals and striving again. Like a Mozart symphony, we create harmonic tensions (the goals) that are resolved in a later musical passage (our achievement of the goals).

Although much has been written about the shortcomings of quarterly goal-oriented management styles, compared with a Japanese style that is more long term and process oriented, little has been said about the constant drive for stability. In most large companies, profound transformation and uncertainty are accepted only for limited periods of time as a means to achieve better ends. Notions of turbulence and chaos in corporate culture are gaining fashion through the writings of management gurus such as Tom Peters, Charles Handy, Margaret Wheatley, Dana Zohar, and Ralph Stacey, yet they are phenomena that most managers avoid. Periods of transformation are accepted only if they are precisely that: periods. At most, large companies are willing to go through phases that shake up the organization if it has grown uncompetitive or if shareholder expectations are not met over a long period.

After many years of below-target returns on equity, Electrolux announced in 1997 that it would undergo extensive restructuring that would involve closure of more than twenty-five sites and the layoff of twelve percent of the total global workforce. This announcement came soon after new management had taken over and provided a window for profound change. The corporate culture at Electrolux had traditionally favored stable and predictable change, which accounted for the period of underperformance followed by a large one-time restructuring. The question that naturally arises in such cases is whether earlier transformation could have avoided such extensive, painful one-time restructuring.

INSTABILITY AND STRESS CAN BE PRODUCTIVE

Few managers today believe that instability should be a permanent way of life for themselves and their organizations. Few espouse that living on the edge with sustained psychological discomfort will lead to better performance for them and their businesses. It is becoming increasingly apparent, however, that in large and complex corporations the ongoing existence of instability in the layers of middle and upper management is increasingly a success factor. Complex systems in unstable environments do not do well with gradual approaches or with approaches that are attempts to force the business into a stable state during phases of instability.

"The bad news is that it is very tiring," said Lafarge vice-chairman Bernard Kasriel, remarking about the stress that his managers bear from sustained instability. "The good news is that it is very motivating." The challenge for the company's leaders is to create enough discomfort for learning and productivity to be optimized. Too much stress leads to demotivation, neglect of work, and ultimately paralysis; not enough can lead to complacency.

THE FIVE KEY ACTIONS

The following five key actions taken together are designed to find a workable balance to achieve the right level of creative tension and organizational instability.

1. Let People Know the Company's Competitive Environment Is Cruel and Unpredictable

Don't overprotect people from the hard realities of the marketplace. When Jean Peyrelevade, the incoming chairman of the once nearly bankrupt French bank Credit Lyonnais, held managers at all levels directly responsible for the difficulties the bank was experiencing, he did the opposite of what many observers expected. Rather than reassuring his personnel by pointing his finger at a few key senior managers, Peyrelevade imposed enough pressure on the entire organization to turn things around. By openly communicating the full nature of a company's difficulties in relation to financial market expectations and industry best practices, a chief executive officer can induce a highly productive, but difficult, work environment.

2. Publicize Individual Successes and Failures while Providing Support for Those Who Have Failed because of Factors beyond Their Control

In companies in which no one is fired for poor performance, people have a high stake in doing the minimum necessary. Such corporate cultures tend to support the status quo and evolve by means of replication rather than transformation. In companies in which people are asked to bear sustained stress and take on above-average challenges, they expect above-average rewards for success and to be treated fairly in case of failure. A simple rule during profound transformation is to identify and raise the visibility of the twenty percent who will lead the change (the change agents) and the twenty percent who cannot or do not wish to contribute to the change program (the resistors). Doing so generally pushes the middle sixty percent in the right direction.

3. Encourage Conflicting Viewpoints as an Ongoing Process Not Just a Reengineering Exercise

Corporate cultures with strong traditions, such as IBM in the late 1970s, tend to discourage opposing viewpoints. Conformity of thinking and values and conformity of symbols such as dress codes, language, and seating plans can stifle valuable opposing ideas that are advance warnings of needed transformation. Intolerance of challenging managers outside traditional hierarchical relations also suppresses opportunities for building fresh perspectives. As part of IBM's overall comeback strategy, Lou Gerstner introduced greater diversity of opinion and style after his arrival at the computer giant in 1993.

4. Produce a Shared Vision of the Objectives to Be Achieved and Communicate It Extensively

Without a widely understood vision, perpetual transformation devolves into an anything goes change program. As uncertainty and stress become endemic, people tend to lose their references and develop anxiety about their personal situations. Senior management plays a key role in stating the company's overarching goal, in listening to individual concerns, in monitoring management processes, and in communicating a sense of direction. This is not the same thing as announcing a priori conceptions of strategy and tactics. It is possible, for example, to fix a goal of achieving an eighteen percent return on net assets or a doubling of the stock price without fixing the particular actions through which to achieve these targets. Chief executive officers such as Jack Welch of General Electric Co. and Colin Marshall of British Airways have shown it is possible to define a new vision and structure for a large (and initially underperforming) company in ways that are widely understood by all without stifling the creativity and self-organization of the people.

5. Provide a Clear Set of Metrics and Report on the Change Taking Place

If you can't measure it, you can't control it. Many companies provide reporting and controlling systems designed by the financial or information systems staff. Such systems often are legacy. They are no longer relevant but have become part of the folklore of the company. The result is stacks and stacks of reports, data sheets, printouts, questionnaires, studies, and other documents that are either ignored or complied with but not used. A second risk is that dysfunctional transformative processes or unexpected results are not communicated to the right people at the right time. Too great a respect for hierarchical lines can block vital information at a middle management level.

Metrics and management reports have to be *re*conceived on a regular basis. As a rule, the relevant information for most managers can be contained in a few simple pages. Even extensive financial reporting on costs and sales need not be impossible for line managers. The best approach to productive instability is an overall package. A constant reworking of action plans combined with tight financial controls on resources can work only if a well-understood vision and a commensurate level of salary and benefits are linked to results. Managers forced to make autonomous decisions (i.e., without much corporate or external support) in uncertain and rapidly changing environments will be effective only if the measures of success are clear.

Box 13.1 The Five Actions That Lead to Implementing Principle IX: Use Organizational Instability to Catalyze Learning

1. Let people know the company's competitive environment is cruel and unpredictable.
2. Publicize individual successes and failures while providing support for those who have failed because of factors beyond their control.
3. Encourage conflicting viewpoints as an ongoing process not just a reengineering exercise.
4. Produce a shared vision of the objectives to be achieved and communicate it extensively.
5. Provide a clear set of metrics and report on the change taking place.

Chapter 14

Principle X. Reenvision Leading: From Command and Control to (R)Evolutionary Influence

Leaders traditionally have been seen as overachievers who set direction, make the key decisions, and energize the troops. These people were viewed in some sense as emerging from a darwinian process of natural selection to become top dog or captains of industry because of their superior managerial capabilities. Once these leaders are installed, their authority has been used primarily to address big issues and give directives, both written and oral, that extend down through the ranks. This conventional view of leadership is deeply rooted in an individualistic and nonsystemic view of the world.

The term *command and control* captures this traditional leadership style with its military connotation and sense of authority and determinism. Heroic leaders are supposed to have all the answers and single-handedly assume all responsibility for the performance of their units or companies. Even the terminology of leader and follower, boss and subordinate is laden with value judgments about roles. Leaders are responsible, competent, and certain in their fiefdom; followers are relatively passive, delegate upward, and are concerned primarily with keeping the trains running on time.

In complex and unstable environments in which organizational learning is the primary source of growth and productivity gain, the role of leadership centers on more subtle tasks. In a learning organization, leaders are visionaries who understand and promote a future that is impossible in the current context. They are team players who actively distribute decision-making power across hierarchical lines and to the frontline. They communicate extensively and manage information flow as a tool for empowerment. They solve problems collaboratively and take the broadest possible view of their actions. The term *(r)evolutionary influence* is used to capture these qualities. The evolution of complex systems is guided by probabilistic influence rather than deterministic control. When discontinuities arise, leaders must occasion a revolution by declaring a future others may not see as possible, and get alignment in the organization so that actions forward that future.

Perpetual transformation requires a shift in role for the top leadership and for all managers entrusted with executive power. Moving from command and control to (r)evolutionary influence is about such a role shift specific to complex and unstable environments. Through (r)evolutionary influence leaders build organizations in which people continuously expand their capabilities to understand the direction the company must take, to share responsibility for decision making, to work with parts of the organization not directly above or below them, and to execute the actions most relevant to the business as a whole.

Peter Senge in *The Fifth Discipline* interviewed Ray Stata, president and chief executive officer of Analog Devices, Inc., a large U.S. corporation in the field of computer components, on the subject of leadership. Stata said:

> The new job description of leaders will involve design of the organization and its policies. This will require seeing the company as a system in which the parts are not only internally connected, but also connected to the external environment, and clarifying how the whole system can work better.[1]

Charles Handy in *The Age of Unreason* reported similar discussions with chief executive officers in his section on leadership:

> I asked someone who had just become chairman of a great multinational what it felt like to be head of one of the world's largest businesses, to be, in one sense, one of our biggest businessmen. "It isn't like that," he replied, "I have just moved round the table and I'm temporarily chairing the team because someone has to."[2]

These descriptions of leadership imply a more egalitarian view of power structures inside a company. Power to effect the future exists throughout an organization not only at the top. The difference between a senior executive and a frontline employee is no longer so great. The senior executive can admit uncertainty and lack of relevant knowledge; the frontline employee can be uniquely positioned to partake in an executive decision.

This is also quite different from conventional notions of decentralization in management theory, which emphasize the role of senior management in making long-term decisions, delegating tasks, and leaving implementation to the parts. In the new view, leadership has a doubly important role: to address major issues and to actively create the conditions for self-learning and distributed decision making so that the entire organization can participate in addressing the major issues.

(R)evolutionary influence does not imply weak leadership. We are not advocating that the chief executive officer adopt a role of teacher, facilitator, or cheerleader and leave the organization largely alone to make participatory decisions. Just because decision-making power is diffused throughout an organization does not mean that senior management does not have a unique capability (and responsibility) to shape strategy, organization, and execution. The chief executive officer remains a symbol of greatness and through his or her charisma is able to motivate others to action.

There are relatively few management styles in which leadership is able to effectively balance the need for centralized authority and the conditions for distributed decision making and self-learning. One source of inspiration, quoted by Yoshio Maruta, chairman of the giant Kao Corporation, was penned by Prince Shotoku in the seventh century. The last of seventeen articles, which the Prince intended as a code of conduct for all Japanese, states unequivocally that decisions on important matters should not be made by one man alone; they should be discussed with many. Because, as the first article says, "Concord is to be honored, and discord to be averted. . . . When concord and union are maintained between those above and below, and harmony rules in the discussion of affairs, the right reason of things will prevail by itself. Then what could not be accomplished?"

Whenever key decisions are to be made in Kao Corporation, Maruta calls in the executives of all the major departments. Those who are at headquarters convene in a simple room furnished with three large tables and chairs; those who are out of town are at the other end of a telephone or video-conferencing facility. There is no paper, no agenda, and no formal procedure. The issues are presented by the chief executive officer, and discussion follows. The average time to reach consensus on handling the issues, Maruta claims, is between five and ten minutes. If the discussion continues for an hour or more, the issue is dropped because there is something fundamentally wrong.

Such a management style works well in Japan, where respect and authority for superiors is inculcated in the national cultural heritage. The sense of sacrifice, the intense loyalty to a single company, and the unquestioning work ethic provided Japanese companies with undoubted advantages after the Second World War. These very qualities, however, also have limited some of the creativity and entrepreneurial ability that lie at the heart of perpetual transformation.

FOUR KEY ACTIONS

What are the elements of the (r)evolutionary influence leadership style advocated here? The following key actions provide guidelines to leading in complex and unstable environments.

1. Be Willing to Take On the Impossible

Transformative change involves getting to a place most people consider impossible to reach when they view it in the traditional context. Declaring an impossible future and committing to its realization is at the center of executive reinvention (another term for transformation at the individual level). It has recently been described by a number of very articulate writers and management consultants, including Tracy Goss in her 1996 book *The Last Word on Power: Executive Reinvention for Leaders Who Must Make the Impossible Happen* (Doubleday, New York, 1996), Peter Roche and Solange Perret of The London Perret Roche Group, and Alex Cohen of the executive education program at Babson College. Our purpose here is not to repeat or summarize this work but to emphasize a few of its key insights. The first is that transformative leadership requires recognizing and stepping outside our innate perspectives on how things really are. Taking on the impossible means accepting that we can make things happen even if the present and the past tell us we cannot. The second insight is that we must be willing to accept a much higher risk for failure in the future. Perpetual transformation means living and working in an environment of ongoing uncertainty, offering great possibilities for success but also considerable risk for failure. Taking a careful and methodical approach to conserving what we have and minimizing future risks may be the riskier approach in complex and unstable environments. The third insight is that for most of us the natural inclination since childhood is to search for control, to call the shots, and to be certain and safe. It takes considerable conscious effort to overcome our inherent command-and-control mind-set. You cannot successfully reinvent an organization without first reinventing the leaders.

2. Create a Work Environment of Mutual Influence

Leaders take the initiative to change the expectations of everyone in the organization so that an atmosphere of partnership exists. Subordinates are no longer passive followers but fully vested members of the team. These ideas are not new; they are only more urgent. Our experience in large multinational organizations is that although lip service often is paid to participatory management and other styles of mutual influence, the reality is otherwise. Leaders are aloof, superior, and heroic, and subordinates feel frustrated in their attempts to communicate their ideas and influence decisions upward.

Changing expectations requires additional skills, such as listening hard to what people think at all levels of the organization. Rigid and formal flows of information have to be replaced by real dialogues in which leaders seek to be influenced by team members at all levels, in turn influencing them with the knowledge acquired.

3. Use Conflict as a Source of Breakthrough

During periods of turbulence, leaders often try to smooth things over by protecting their people from change or discontinuity. Just as they often avoid radical change for their companies, they suppress conflict between team members. Yet in the transformation process, conflict has value in getting the tough issues on the table. Conflict is a way to pierce through existing problems and allows a team to move on to radically new issues.

4. Keep the Largest View Possible

A particular aspect of complexity in business is the interconnectedness of every part of a business with all other parts. Leaders have a special role in linking decisions in a particular area to the larger context in which that area exists. Managers often forget that what is good for their units may not be in the best interest of their company. Actions that negatively affect one area can be to the overall good of the company.

The largest view possible depends on where one is sitting. Leaders operate at multiple levels, as shown in Figure 14.1. A bank employee at a local branch may lead a team to reduce credit issuance delays, whereas John Browne, chairman of British Petroleum, may help determine the rate at which global oil fields will be explored in the twenty-first century. Figure 14.1 shows that leaders at each level of industry have a corresponding larger view that takes into account the interests of the broader context in which the leader operates.

The ability of complex systems to survive depends largely on the quality of their interconnections and relations with the larger environment in which they operate. A department manager who pursues only the interests of his or her

Level	Larger view	Leader
Employee	→ Team	Employee
Team	→ Department	Team manager
Department	→ Operating unit	Department manager
Operating unit	→ Company	Operating unit manager
Company	→ Industry	CEO
Industry	→ Society and ecology	CEO of industry leader

Figure 14.1 The Larger View Depends on Where You Are in the Organization

immediate team can achieve good results during straight-forward and predictable times. When the entire industry is undergoing radical transformation, however, positive results for the team depend on coordinated management with other departments and players outside the company.

Box 14.1 The Four Actions Specific to Principle X: Reenvision Leading—From Command and Control to (R)Evolutionary Influence

1. Be willing to take on the impossible.
2. Create a work atmosphere of mutual influence.
3. Use conflict as a source of breakthrough.
4. Keep the largest view possible.

Chapter 15

Managing Information: A Key to Successful Implementation

TRANSFORMATION AND INFORMATION SYSTEMS

Information management is increasingly critical to the process of transformation. We need, however, to start with a basic question: What is meant by the word *information*? In the new science, the notion of information is intimately linked with the degree of complexity of a system. One mathematical definition of the complexity of a system measures the amount of information necessary to describe that system with a universal computer such as the Turing machine. The more information required by a system, the more complex it is.

In the corporate world, we have a tendency to separate information from systems of information. Systems of information are assimilated to information technology (IT) or management information systems—those highly technical computer and communication black boxes that run operating and application software. Yet the word *information* covers a much larger field, from numerical data to document text and from images to the spoken word. Information thus covers both data handled by information systems and the myriad of other forms of communication and data storage inside a corporation.

THE STRUCTURING ROLE OF INFORMATION IN COMPLEX SYSTEMS

Chaos and complexity theory in the natural sciences have focused on information flows within complex systems and the role played by these flows in structuring, sustaining, and helping to make the system evolve. Complex systems can be unstable and ordered at the same time. A useful image is the human pyramid formed by circus acrobats. Each performer is continuously adjusting his or her muscles in response to the movements of all the other performers—the pyramid is perpetually in motion. Although lacking stability, such systems have a dynamic order of their own.

Insights from the new sciences reveal that streams of information (or energy in natural systems) are responsible for imposing dynamic order. For example, thermodynamic experiments with liquids show that a steadily increasing source of heat causes increasing turbulence and distinct structures suddenly form in the liquid, the so-called Bernoulli cells. Further increasing the heat source causes the cells to vanish and the turbulence to reappear. Chaos modeling shows that all states between order and disorder are possible in complex systems, that information flow can switch the system from one state to another at critical thresholds.

Drawing lessons from these new-science insights into the role of information is useful for managers facing high degrees of complexity inside their companies. In complex environments, the optimum transfer of information cannot occur within totally defined structures, nor can it occur without any structure at all. Order and disorder are both to be avoided when it comes to designing information systems in fast-changing and complex corporate environments. The rigidity of the first is as useless as the total lack of structure in the second.

INFORMATION TECHNOLOGY AS CATALYST OF THE PROCESS OF TRANSFORMATION

Inside corporations today, information is intimately associated with IT. Information is the content. Information systems define the structure of the circulation of information and become the means to diffuse and treat information. It is no wonder that diffusion and treatment of information have changed dramatically in recent times given the exponential progress in IT itself. IT is becoming the backbone of the corporate functioning, and it has rapidly become a tool to rethink and redesign the process of doing business. Companies are transforming their delivery platforms to e-everything: e-customer, e-supplier, and even e-employee, as technology makes virtual commerce possible.

Consider how Procter & Gamble sells products such as toothpaste and diapers to retailer Wal-Mart. IT allows P&G to control its production and delivery schedule to Wal-Mart, manage its receivables, and analyze sales information. IT also has allowed P&G to change the *way* in which it sells these products to Wal-Mart. Rather then sending a sales representative to every Wal-Mart store to evaluate use of shelf space and complete order forms with a Wal-Mart buyer, P&G uses a computerized interface to communicate directly with its factories. The result is decreased sales and procurement costs, increased quality, faster cycles, lower stock, and a host of associated benefits. In the personal computer industry, Dell revolutionized the sales process with its direct-marketing approach. Bargain-basement retailers such as emachines have responded with Web-based assembly and sales strategies of their own.

IT and information management have become the active drivers of change in terms of innovation and transformation. They are factors of discontinuity (intended or not), they are means to optimizing business processes, and they are at the heart of perpetual transformation. We turn now to two illustrations in consumer goods and in the travel industry.

THE CONSUMER GOODS INDUSTRY

Defined here as the manufacture and sale of all products (foods, clothes, appliances, and so on) purchased by the individual consumer, this industry includes suppliers of raw materials, producers, wholesale distributors, and retailers. Examples of leading companies include Unilever, Procter & Gamble, Japan Tobacco, and Carrefour, all ranked in the global Fortune 200. Producers, the primary focus of this section, are in the middle of the value-added chain and must resolve questions of procurement of raw materials, manufacturing, marketing, and logistics and meet the needs of individual consumers.

The needs of individual consumers are constantly undergoing change. Tastes evolve; yesterday's styling is no longer in demand. Expectations continue to rise concerning product performance and price-quality value. Consumers are less and less faithful to one supplier; they don't hesitate to switch brands. The developed country market (defined as the members of the Organization for Economic Cooperation and Development) is no longer in a high growth phase. Demand during the 1990s has shadowed growth of the gross national product for these countries, averaging one to two percent per year. Competition is becoming increasingly global and intense. Wholesale distributors such as Home Depot and Wal-Mart stores, with annual sales in the tens of billions of dollars, have amassed considerable purchasing power and drive increasingly hard bargains with producers that involve price, product quality, product marketing, and consumer services.

In the face of this increasingly complex, fast-changing, and competitive industrial environment, producers are reevaluating their strategic positioning. They are looking to change the rules of the game to their advantage. The leading

consumer goods producers are undertaking perpetual transformation approaches in which IT is playing a primordial
role. IT, they hope, will allow their strategic positions to
evolve from purchasers of raw materials and suppliers of
finished goods to one of dynamic partnership with all players
in the value-added chain, including the final consumer. This
new partnership role, if implemented correctly, should allow
producers to regain a measure of control in the fast-changing
consumer goods industry.

Past Information Flows in the Consumer Goods Industry

Until now, the value-added chain was composed of activities
that were poorly interlinked. Players knew only their immediate suppliers and customers. A raw-materials supplier dealt
only with the plant to whom it sold. The plant's relations were
limited to raw-materials suppliers, the sales department, and
the wholesaler distributor. Retail stores did not interface with
either the raw-materials supplier or the manufacturing plant.
This model is shown in Figure 15.1.

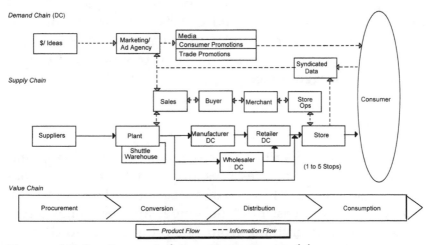

Figure 15.1 Current Industry Operating Model

Factors for Success in the Consumer Goods Industry

Four key success factors are generally identified for success in the consumer goods industry—time to market, distributor relations, resource management of diversity, and delivered cost. Before we look at how IT is used to create dynamic partnerships for the producers, we briefly review each key success factor.

Time to Market

As demand changes it is imperative for producers of consumer goods to follow suit. This need to satisfy evolving end-user tastes can cover several different aspects. It can correspond to an emerging niche market or an underlying trend, such as the growth in the seniors (sixty-five years and older) population or the demand for green (ecologically safe) products. For example, most western food distributors offer farm-grown produce guaranteed to be free of preservatives, coloring agents, artificial flavoring, and other added chemicals. The continuing cola wars have brought a host of new-age drinks with innovative mixes and packaging to satisfy generation X around the world. Pepsi's ill-fated Michael Jackson campaign and Coke's new formula, including caffeine-free, cherry-taste, and sugar-free varieties, were part of this challenge to bring the right products to the right markets at the right time.

Distributor Relations

The demands of distributors and retailers are growing and adding to traditional pressures imposed by the final consumer. The traditional image of a distributor looking to buy a product for the best price no longer applies. Today's distributors want everything from in-store logistics to data on orders, marketing support, and an ability to deal directly with final customer inquiries. Producers differentiate themselves with services and information as much as with product supply.

Resource Management of Diversity

Increased product ranges necessitate flexible manufacturing capability. Except in instances in which specialized production lines are possible, a producer has to build in the ability to switch from one type of product (for example, high-end, color, multicomponent) to another (economy, white, single component) and do so as a function of incoming information about use of shelf space in client-distributor stores. To this variety of products are routinely added a range of packages: the two-pack, the kid-pack, the special-event pack. For still other products, a need might exist to respect temperature or other special transport or storage conditions.

Delivered Cost

Producers continue, as they always have, to focus on controlling their total delivered costs, from materials procurement to manufacturing, packaging, logistics, and overhead. Volume and experience play an important role in keeping unit fixed costs to a minimum. Competitive advantage in costs translates into better margins, which can be used to invest in product quality and customer service.

Use of Information Technology to Create Dynamic Partnerships

For producers to excel in the four key success factors and counter increasingly difficult competitive conditions, a complete business transformation has been undertaken. Leading companies have begun to restructure the value-added chain and to rethink their links with the different types of players. Their primary implementation tool is IT. The starting point has been to improve the level of information flow between raw-materials suppliers, producers, wholesalers, and retailers. Information systems have been linked with emphasis on adopting compatible computer and software technologies and on common data formats. Data itself has been reorganized and managed at the level of the value-added chain rather than at the level of the individual company. Information is thus structured to allow decision making to account for the needs of the producer's partners as well as its own needs. Computerized order-delivery links directly to retail cashiers, for example, allow producers to improve planning of their production runs, reduce stock, perceive new trends earlier, and saves retailers costs associated with completing orders the old way.

The new information systems are conceived to maximize flexibility and adaptability to yet unforeseen future changes. New products or new production technologies should not require a complete revision of the information system, but merely adjustments. Beyond linkages with other players in the industry, these information systems seek to include the final consumer. The Internet is being used increasingly as a sales tool. Real-time consumer input is used in modeling demand and marketing decision models. These IT tools allow producers to focus on the value created for consumers and ultimately lead to greater customer satisfaction and higher profits.

Leading-edge Information Flows in the Consumer Goods Industry

New IT systems have allowed a reduction in the number of intermediaries and an increase in the number of information links to all players. The result has brought producers into closer partnership with the rest of the industry and has offered them a greater degree of control over the highly competitive and fast-changing market. Interrelations between industry players have become more numerous and more intense. All the players feed and use the information system thereby created.

Future Industry Operating Model

The information produced at the industry level allows each player to better assess the returns on their investments and their individual profit and loss performance. Operations are no longer considered as actions that can be isolated; instead a degree of coordination allows players to pull together toward satisfying the final customer.

Dynamic partnerships in the consumer goods industry have been facilitated by new global-applications software, such as those distributed by SAP, Oracle, and Baan. These IT tools allow producers to measure the value added of individual operations within the overall customer satisfaction process. Efficiency and flexibility increase, as does transparency in the assessment of profits and costs. New IT-driven partnerships allow producers of consumer goods to lead transformation in their own companies and to influence transformation in their industry. This model is illustrated in Figure 15.2.

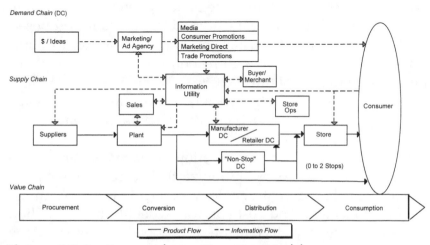

Figure 15.2 Future Industry Operating Model

THE TRAVEL INDUSTRY

The travel agency business has undergone considerable transformation pushed by large corporate clients with specific
executive travel needs and the growth in global tourism
and transportation. In its traditional role of making telephone
reservations and issuing tickets, the travel agency seemed
destined for the corporate graveyard. Airline companies and
hotels are providing such services directly to the final
customer. American Airlines, for example, has launched
it own electronic order system. Reservations and ticketing
are increasingly done through global distribution systems
previously reserved for agency use. Sabre is now accessible on the Internet. The practice of sending a courier
across town to deliver travel tickets will soon be obsolete.
Special printers linked to central reservation systems will
allow corporate clients to print their own tickets directly in
the office.

Travel agencies have had to reposition themselves using
IT and information system management. Pushed by the need
of large corporate clients anxious to control executive travel
costs, these agencies are becoming financial advisors. Agencies are evolving from destination consultant and ticket issuer
into providers of cost management systems. Which large
enterprise is able to follow the myriad tariff systems proposed
by the major airlines? Which organization wants to audit
travel costs? Agencies able to respond to this emerging corporate need to control travel costs are finding new and potentially profitable activity. Some agencies are offering to manage
the accounting requirements of corporate clients with
application-specific software.

Advances in IT and information management are allowing travel agencies to revolutionize their core competencies.
Agencies are becoming technology experts in travel planning,
data management, and cost control. Rosenbluth, a $3 billion
U.S. travel agency, has made its global IT network the
centerpiece of its strategy. Personalized service is offered to

individual employees of corporate clients through a communication platform accessible twenty-four hours a day.

Technological prowess requires considerable financial investment. To succeed players have to be big to exploit economies of scale. The mergers of Havas and American Express and of Carlson and Wagonlits are examples of industry consolidation driven by technological investment. Carlson manages a technology division that recently grew from four hundred fifty to five hundred fifty people on the global level. The division includes IT specialists working on projects such as Web-TV, which allows users to access the Internet on television via cable operators.

Havas and American Express have launched their own reservations system on the Internet dedicated to corporate users. Via Voyages is creating a virtual agency that will use the French electronic network Minitel. Clients will be able to make and modify electronic reservations by computer. Such services are provided in addition to the battery of specific software packages that will be offered to analyze costs and follow expense accounts.

New Entrants

Technology differentiation is providing a host of incentives for new competitors, many of whom are coming from outside the travel industry. The value added of agencies has changed. The constant drive of corporate clients to control expenses and analyze travel usage favors financial and IT heavyweights such as American Express and Andersen Consulting.

The three emerging competencies are reservations management, electronic client interface, and upstream cost control. Andersen Consulting through its subsidiary Via World Com already has sixty workers and a Web site dedicated to business travelers. Other new entrants include EDS through its reservations network subsidiary System One and, to no one's surprise, Microsoft. Allied with World Span and

American Express, Bill Gates is looking at ways to create a virtual agency on the Web through Microsoft Expedia.

THE NEW INTERNET TECHNOLOGIES

The Internet is an ensemble of computers linked together by specific lines of communication. The system was initially developed by the U.S. government to bring together the major computing centers. The idea was to maintain a distributed nervous system on the continent in case one or more computer centers were damaged in a nuclear attack. Very quickly scientists around the world took advantage of the network to link new computers. As additional users were connected, a living network of scientific institutions, universities, governments, companies, and individuals created a novel way of communication.

As it is today, the Internet is not only the sum total of its users; it also is defined by initial connection rules. These standards for connection and communication, such as *http,* allow the Internet to maintain coherence at the global level. Connections to the Internet were initially limited to universities, research centers, and government agencies. The Internet existed for more than two decades more or less in this form. Only in the 1990s did it experience explosive growth. Millions of personal computers were hooked up directly or through local area networks to central computers that were connected to the Internet.

The growth of the Internet changed its purpose. Users were no longer mainly scientists and academics. Individual users and companies in search of productivity improvements turned to the Internet for electronic books and documents, raw data, menus, meeting minutes, advertisements, video and audio recordings, and transcripts of interactive conversations. As the purpose of the Internet changed, so did the technology. From standardized connection formats and tools evolved software development tools such as Java, browsers such as Netscape, and a host of application-specific programs. The ability to access and communicate a broad range of information from a computer terminal changed the way companies looked at their business activity. No longer a simple communication tool, the Internet has become a separate reality.

Box 15.1   The Spectacular Growth of the Internet: Number of Internet Servers

The number of hosts grew an average of 118 percent per year over the fifteen-year period between 1983 and 1998. (See Figure 15.3 for the period of 1995 to 1998.)

The United States, Canada, and have the most Internet connections (in 1999 more than thirty percent of the adult population was connected either at work or at home).

Singapore, Russia, Brazil, Finland, Japan, Israel, Poland, Taiwan, and Ireland were the highest growth markets over this period.

Sources: IDC, Internet

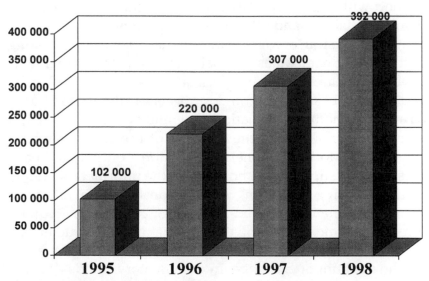

Figure 15.3 New Internet Server Hardware Units
Source: IDC, Alex Brown & Sons

The Internet represents a technological discontinuity with the past to the extent that it presents radically different possibilities for buying and selling products and services, marketing, procurement, payment, and most other business activities. Major insurance companies create Web sites that allow them to make account transactions from any connected personal computer. Tourist agencies use the Internet to reach individual clients for destinations around the world. Individuals have voice communication over the Internet by means of digitally encoded speech. This capability enables them to bypass long distance telephone companies.

The Internet is more than a new means of communication or a way to lower information costs. Beyond these basic functions, the Internet is a technology that obliges companies to rethink and in many cases redesign their organizations. Virtual access to customers without geographic borders has led many multinational organizations, particularly high-technology players such as IBM and Oracle, to remodel their organizations around the Internet. Each person, function, and operating unit is linked independently to every other without a centralizing structure. Every part of the organization can connect with the exterior environment of clients, competitors, financial analysts, and other business partners.

The physical borders that separate persons, operating units, and the companies themselves from their environments have disappeared. In many cases, a company may be legally and financially separate from a supplier or distributor, but in terms of economic information flow and work performed, it is inseparable. Consider the example of Procter & Gamble's factory links to its customers' retail stores or Toyota's partnership with suppliers. In both cases, the information system is the enabling factor in the relationship. The effect on the bottom line is measured in terms of cycle time, accuracy, direct costs, and delayering of rigid hierarchical structures.

The nonmaterial nature of information has consequences for the medium of exchange. In early history, goods and services were bartered. Later the medium became unit weights of a commodity such as rice or precious metal such as gold. Coins with a face value backed by government decree have been in use since Roman times. Much later came paper currency. Today transactions between large financial institutions are purely numerical data transfers. Walter Wriston, long-time head of Citicorp Bank, considers that the information standard has de facto replaced the dollar and gold standard as the basis for international finance.

Currency denominations are conventions. They have no physical reality other than the confidence of markets in the issuing institution, typically a national central bank. If Microsoft tomorrow issued a virtual currency created specially for Internet transactions, and if user confidence were sufficiently great, the currency could become a denomination to rival major currencies. The implications for fiscal control, money laundering, inflation, and the like are beyond the scope of our analysis, but the possibility of such a virtual currency is easily conceivable. If the industrial revolution ushered in the era of paper currency, the advent of the Internet could well signal the birth of virtual currency.

INDIVIDUALIZED MASS MARKETING BECOMES POSSIBLE

During most of the twentieth century, companies had a choice of commercial approaches: personalized shop or phone pitches corresponding to individual needs or mass marketing popularized by supermarkets. Each approach corresponded to a distinct set of economics (margins, volumes) that existed for every socioeconomic layer of the market. Rich and poor buy their products from mass marketers. Each of us also is pleased to spend a little more at the corner grocery store or fashion boutique where we are known by name.

The Internet has obliterated the dichotomy between mass marketing and person-to-person selling. The World Wide Web allows companies to have direct and personal contact with each potential customer. Data collected over the Web provides detailed profiles of buying habits, tastes, and financial means. Made-to-measure selling with broad product ranges and mass volumes suddenly is possible. The Internet allows companies to follow the life cycles of consumers, to identify credit problems and employment changes, birthdays, and weddings. Client segmentation is revolutionized; the global village becomes virtual. Specialized companies such as Conso-Data are exploiting the segmentation potential. Through surveys it collects information on the tastes and habits of millions of households. With the information it generates sophisticated marketing analyses and market segmentations, which are then sold to other companies.

THE VIRTUAL ORGANIZATION

A growing number of multinational companies are adapting to the new information technologies in ways radically different from those used in the past. Geographic proximity often is irrelevant; knowledge-based competence, wherever it exists, is key. Project teams dispersed on continents work together in real time. Communication is by means of telephone conferencing, voice mail, video conferencing, netmetings, and e-mail. Executive travel continues to be important, but it assumes a different character. Face-to-face meetings are used to create personalized bonds, assist in making key decisions, and send organizational messages about priorities and commitments. A virtual organization in high-tech industries is a matter of survival when products and markets can change overnight and across continents. When making a sale depends on several different and geographically scattered competencies, virtual organization allows a company to propose client-specific solutions independently from the number and location of the parties involved.

KEY ACTIONS IN INFORMATION MANAGEMENT

Information technology has revolutionized the way companies do business. Electronic data exchanges are now the norm;

financial flow is handled in real time; mass marketing is made to measure; virtual organizations link partners in different continents. As a result of these changes information and IT have come to be considered strategic resources not overhead or support. As complexity rises in the competitive environment, senior management itself acquires a new role: guarantor of the company's openness and accessibility to relevant information. Keeping an organization up-to-date and efficient in its use of information is no longer a question for IT specialists. In the following section we look at seven key actions for furthering a strategic approach to information systems and technology.

SEVEN KEY ACTIONS

1. Design Information Flows That Serve the Overall Business Rather than Piecemeal Functions

Information flows are at the very heart of the business activity. In financial services, whether they are provided by banks, insurance companies, or capital markets, information *is* the business activity. In manufacturing industries, information systems provide crucial support to finance, controlling, sales and procurement, research and development, logistics, and general management. Without effective information systems, companies lose a key competitive edge in the process of transformation. This is because information serves the overall business purpose not piecemeal functions. The overall business purpose is supported by a wide variety of IT roles including the following:

- Databases in marketing, research and development, and accounts receivable
- All of the company's financial reporting, including accounting, controlling, asset management, payroll, budgeting, and investing
- Executive information systems designed to assist in managerial decision making

- Transactions between the company and its customers
- Relations between the company and the outside financial community of banks, financial analysts, and shareholders
- Relations between the company and other industry partners
- Performance measurement systems, including compensation and career advancement
- Industrial information systems that ensure manufacturing process control

Box 15.2   Information Systems in Insurance Companies

An insurance company operates as a giant information center. A large part of the available information often unexploitable because it exists in multiple information systems that are not compatible among themselves. The new information technologies offer solutions that allow the systems to communicate. They also provide tools for delving into the mass of information to extract only what is needed, when it is needed, and in the form in which it is needed.

In these conditions, the choice of IT platform quickly becomes a key strategic decision. It goes well beyond the technical questions raised by IT specialists. Senior management must be closely involved because the company's transformation capacity is at stake. In conventional organizational structures, IT departments are responsible for choosing the computer hardware and software and often for formatting data and deciding which reports can technically be generated. The overdelegation of information management to IT specialists has lead to some serious distortions. In one division of Lafarge, a combination of folklore and insistence by IT specialists that long-standing computer printouts could not be changed led hard-line managers to focus on the wrong indicators. The result was that a number of sales were made below cost, some warehouse terminals were operated at sustained losses, and operating unit performance was inaccurately evaluated. In other examples FedEx lost several hundred million dollars on its zap-mail project, and a bug in American Airlines' yield management cost $15 million in lost revenue.

The time is past when IT managers could explain to the head of sales or a plant manager that the information needed could not be provided as asked for. With the IT tools currently available, technological barriers to efficient information management no longer exist. Complexity and rapid, discontinuous change necessitate that companies stay on the leading edge of information management.

2. Focus on the Relevance of Information

Garbage in, garbage out. When the flow of information inside a company contains superfluous elements or is not relevant to objectives, the entire management process loses credibility. People feel less motivated to achieve and end up ignoring the mass of information they receive. In determining the relevance of information, it is essential to involve senior management (for objectives, financial targets, key indicators, and methods of measurement) and front-line employees. The ultimate users must be convinced about the value of the information in their day-to-day work. Without a voice about the substance, format, and timing of information, front-line workers are unlikely to exploit the information to the fullest extent.

At every level in a company, too much information is undesirable because it draws unnecessary resources into sorting and analyzing. Excess information can lead to the creation of parallel underground systems to expedite decisions. Too little information also can be catastrophic for a company facing rapid and discontinuous change. Senior management needs to be involved in an ongoing effort to review the relevance of the information being circulated throughout the organization. Folklore reporting and diffusion that exist because they have always existed must be weeded out and new information sought out as business realities change.

3. Avoid One-way Flows of Information

Inside large corporate organizations, separate departments exist to manage various kinds of information, such as manufacturing process control, order delivery, accounting, and payroll. Each department needs data input from other parts of the organization. Controllers need cost data from the operating units; procurement specialists need product-formula and volume data from manufacturing; production planning needs sales and logistics data to determine run lengths and capacity utilization. Management of information goes beyond these basic procedures. Procurement, planning, production, and financing are integral parts of the interlocking transformation process. When one activity changes, the rest of the company adjusts in search of what in the science of thermodynamics is called *dynamic nonstable equilibrium*. Each entity acts and reacts to information generated by other entities in the system, yet the whole maintains coherence over time. Consider the case of a consumer goods manufacturer with a planned production site to be financed locally in a country that suddenly experiences high real interest rates. Economic forecasts of macroeconomic trends and costs of capital, internal manufacturing data on comparative labor costs in other countries, sales data on product pricing, and research and development data on upcoming technology innovations can determine which financial policy is ultimately followed. The possibilities include refinancing from abroad, equity financing, pulling the plug on the planned investment, and short- or long-term hedging on foreign exchange exposure.

Although the concept of information sharing inside large organizations is readily accepted in principle, implementation difficulties continue to plague many companies. Being able to identify customer service innovations in the Hong Kong subsidiary for application in the U.S. market can be a vital source of performance improvement. All too often such knowledge transfers are made partially, late, or not at all. Effective information systems facilitate internal and external performance benchmarking and the establishment and monitoring of best practices. In the current business environment, it is a matter of survival to identify innovations and trends before the rest of the industry does. Without two-way flows of information, each person or unit risks making suboptimal decisions that affect the overall transformation process. This risk is greatly amplified when weak signals of change have the potential to become major events.

4. As Complexity Increases, Increase the Number of Information Interfaces

A core notion developed in the new sciences of chaos and complexity is that as complexity increases, so must the number of information interfaces. As a company diversifies its product range, geographic markets, national cultures, and technologies used, it needs to add interfaces between people, departments, and operating units. This insight comes from the much older science of cybernetics, in which it was stated more than fifty years ago in the so-called law of requisite variety that any system that seeks to cope with variety externally must incorporate variety internally.

Information systems determine the number and quality of interfaces. The ability to create a network of high-quality interfaces is strongly linked to self-organization (see Chapter 11) and to a flatter and more efficient organization (see Chapter 12). Yet obstacles to the diffusion of information are numerous. They are psychological as often as they are real and include turf battles, rigid lines of hierarchical communication, a refusal to be confronted, a need to control information, and occasionally legitimate concerns about confidentiality.

Box 15.3   IBM: The Case of Dysfunctional Marketing Information Systems

In the 1990s IBM went through a difficult period in managing key marketing information systems. The collection and diffusion of information throughout the company was complex and uncoordinated. IBM had forty-nine divisions feeding twenty-seven departments. Within the twenty-seven departments, hundreds of people analyzed data on market segments and competitors. Given the overlap in the data being followed by each department, a large part of the information collected and diffused by one department could have been useful to the other departments. The information was structured in local databases that did not communicate among themselves. In addition, the departments were typically reluctant to share data or search for information that could have been useful to other departments. The reasons for withholding information were numerous, ranging from a lack of time to deal with requests originating outside the department to issues of confidentiality.

Senior management intervened to implement a company-wide information system to analyze markets and competitors throughout the world. More than one million documents from the various internal departments and external sources of marketing information were integrated. The entire database was made accessible with a single search engine.

The results were impressive. The productivity of the new system improved in terms of collection and diffusion by means of eliminating redundancies and waste, and the actual analysis of segments and competitors became vastly more sophisticated. For example, competitor analysis with the new system allowed global identification of emerging technological trends spotted by several different departments within IBM and communication of these trends to all sales departments.

5. Tie Information to Action

Information for the sake of information has no economic justification. The process of collection, analysis, and diffusion consumes time and resources. Furthermore, there is nothing more demotivating for a team whose purpose is to carry out market studies or other database work than to realize that the value of their efforts is negligible. In one case, a development team in eastern Europe spent two years analyzing and proposing investment opportunities in specialty products. For reasons related to the company's lack of commitment to these products and poor organizational functioning, a yard-high stack of studies (some of which were studies by headquarters on the studies made by the field teams) were the only tangible result after twenty-four months. Meanwhile competitors were investing, and the best opportunities were disappearing. Not surprisingly, a key member of the development team who had hoped to take an operational position in the newly created business left the company.

Even functional departments with responsibility for monitoring competitors or technology developments must be actively plugged into the major decision-making circuits. Tying information to action is critical to self-organization. The processes of organizational learning and distributed decision making require a high intensity of information input. Even organizations with more traditional, hierarchical systems of decision making need company-wide information input to make relevant decisions.

6. Use Information to Stimulate Learning

The capability of a company to learn in complex and turbulent environments is depends heavily on the quality of the information available to it. A wide net of information sources, ease of access, pertinent analyses, and a tie-in to action can allow a company to spot emerging trends before competitors do, avoid impending disaster, and serenely pursue a path of permanent, ongoing transformation.

We recall a key insight from the new sciences of chaos and complexity. Information drives the structuring process in complex systems much as sunlight (energy) drives the living process on earth. Although this insight has always applied to companies, it is only in the much more complex and unstable environment of today that the role of information flow becomes visible. As Ray Stata, chief executive officer of Analog Devices, has said, the capacity of a company to learn has become the only durable source of competitive advantage.

Using information to stimulate learning requires a coordinated multiinterfaced system at any given point in time and obliges a company to create a memory of its past. In periods of ongoing change market studies, competitor profiles, technology monitoring, and the like serve a purpose only if the lessons learned are remembered. At points of discontinuous change, these insights from the past must be considered carefully along with more forward-looking thinking to draw conclusions about action. Without a memory of the past, management is faced with reinventing the wheel at each moment in time. Existing information technology allows companies to create integrated databases manipulated with expert systems and decision-making tools to enrich or selectively conserve the company's collective memory. For IT to be used effectively, however, it must be implemented in a cultural context in which learning is valued and information is managed to that end.

George Day, professor of marketing at the Huntsman Center for Global Competition and Innovation of the University of Pennsylvania Wharton School of Management, observed that learning helps managers anticipate change on a permanent basis and to do so faster than competitors. It is no longer sufficient to describe a market in detail or to define with precision the competitive positioning of one's company. A good manager must be able to draw on the accumulated experience of his or her company and anticipate market reactions to actions eventually taken. The success of the proposed actions depends on the quality of the information collected during the initial study phase, on the conceptual framework chosen by senior management to analyze this information, and on the often hidden cultural context of implementation. Companies must be capable of analyzing and anticipating emerging trends and of acting on them. The process of self-learning must allow managers to ask the right questions at the right moment, to integrate probable answers in their understanding of the evolving market, and to share their conclusions and recommendations with other members of the management team.

7. Structure Information Flows to Support Explicitly the Process of Perpetual Transformation

For information to flow efficiently throughout a company, it becomes necessary to define and implement a flow structure. For each person to access and contribute effectively to relevant information, senior management must conceive a flow structure that allows the collection, manipulation, analysis, and diffusion of data in support of perpetual transformation.

Corporate information structures typically classify, screen, and organize information in ways that are the outgrowth of past needs and assumptions. Automatic biases become built into the flow structure. The biases tend to reaffirm data that supports past practices and exclude data that indicates radically different ways of doing business.

Consider the strategic reassessment recently undertaken by Multiplex Corporation, the industrial equipment supplier. The object of this reassessment was to decide how to react in the face of declining margins in several market segments in which the company had historically held a leadership position. During the pioneering phase of the company's business, clients had been relatively insensitive to high prices. As the various market segments matured and competitors emerged, more and more clients began choosing a supplier on the basis of price. Multiplex quickly began to lose market share. Senior management had apparently identified the situation well, but the structure of information flow led to conclusions that hurt the company. Historical assumptions about the attractiveness of high-end market segments, continued growth in demand, and the weak negotiating power of clients allowed middle managers to interpret new information in ways that reaffirmed the company's traditional strategy of retreating to market segments in which customers were still disposed to paying above-average prices. This strategy further invited new competitors, and as the number of high-end segments shrank, Multiplex experienced higher unit costs as utilization of production capacity decreased.

The structure imposed on Multiplex's information flow actually discouraged transformation of the company from high-priced pioneer to a renewed basis of competitive advantage. We have encountered a range of other examples of misaligned information flow structures in large companies. In one case, information flow structures conceived for a capital-intensive, risk-averse, supply-driven business were used for other businesses within the same company. Because these other businesses were marketing and sales driven and had high sales to assets ratios, the slow, procedural, and centralizing information structure of the core business proved to be a handicap. Rather than favoring field reactivity and opportunistic decision making, business development proved far slower than for competitors. The result was poor performance, a growing lack of conviction in the potential for the other businesses to create value, and further reinforcement of slow, procedural, and centralizing information structures. A vicious circle emerged of misaligned information flow leading to poor performance, which reinforced the misalignment of information.

Effective information flow structures necessitate that management make the right choice of hardware and software. IT that does not have built-in flexibility can lead to the biases described earlier. Even as late as the 1980s, IT often did not allow for a global structure for information flow and the capacity for open system architecture. The executive information systems were examples of a relatively rigid architecture that lacked effective implementation in a permanently changing environment. The information system products offered by companies such as SAP or Oracle in the 1990s have largely overcome the limits of the past. It is now for senior managers of large companies to make use of the available technology.

Box 15.4   The Seven Key Actions for Meeting the Challenge of Information Management

1. Design information flows that serve the overall business rather than piecemeal functions.
2. Focus on the relevance of information.
3. Avoid one-way flows of information.
4. As complexity increases, increase the number of information interfaces.
5. Tie information to action.
6. Use information to stimulate self-learning.
7. Structure information flows to support explicitly the process of perpetual transformation.

Chapter 16

Environmental Sustainability: An Extension of the Ten Principles

Multinational companies now face a challenge of transformation that will alter the way the world occurs: the challenge of managing a sustainable environment. Environmental factors increasingly underlie all business activity. Whether companies choose to deal with this challenge is not the question; *not* choosing will produce its own set of results. The results with which we are concerned here are those of shareholder value creation or destruction. Environmental sustainability is first a business proposition and second a good neighbor policy if it is to succeed at all.

The Ten Principles focus on company transformation. They determine the conditions under which companies are able to reinvent themselves on an ongoing basis to change the rules of the game for themselves and their industry when complexity and turbulence are the norm. The challenge of environmental sustainability is different and more fundamental. It defines the capability of a company to alter the outer reality and context of business, which includes market institutions, economic growth, and quality of life.

We offer a prediction: The way in which a small group of people and companies handle environmental sustainability in the next ten to twenty years will abruptly determine whether the global economic system survives and in what form. The key player in this unfolding drama will undoubtedly be private sector enterprise. As Stuart L. Hart of the University of Michigan Business School said, "Like it or not, the responsibility for ensuring a sustainable world falls largely on the shoulders of the world's enterprises, the economic engines of the future. . . . Corporations can and should lead the way, helping to shape public policy and driving change in consumers' behavior. In the final analysis, it makes good business sense."

The capability of leading companies to influence the outer world in which we live will come about only if they can credibly associate environmental performance with shareholder value. Impending environmental thresholds will bring environmental concerns and corporate profit closer together. The visible trend is toward stricter environmental legislation, greener values of consumers and investors, and a growing market demand for environmentally friendly products and services. The predominant mentality of corporate management, however, remains unconcerned with these issues, except when they involve respecting the law and obvious risks to profit. It will take farsighted thinking and the activism of a group of pioneers to lead the way.

Information technology will be the most powerful tool in this battle between corporate growth and profit on the one hand and environmental degradation on the other. For example, Robert Shapiro, chief executive officer of United States–based Monsanto, believes that in the chemicals industry "[information technology] will let us miniaturize things, avoid waste, and produce more value without producing and processing more stuff. The substitution of information for stuff is essential to sustainability."[1]

Environmental sustainability is defined as "an economic state where the demands placed upon the environment by people and commerce can be met without reducing the capacity of the environment to provide for future generations." The challenge for leading companies is to contribute toward such an economic state while continuing to generate the financial value expected by shareholders. Businesses that pursue growth and prosperity must be able to do so without intolerably abusing the environment.

In this chapter we discuss the extent to which global industry leaders are in a position to influence the world's physical and social environment. We also suggest that exercising this influence is a question of emotion, of ethics, and primarily of coldly rational business logic. In other words, it is possible for companies to be good neighbors and make money doing it. Although the measure of success remains traditional cash flow return on investment, formulating and implementing an environmental strategy requires nontraditional thinking.

ENVIRONMENTAL ISSUES CAN DRIVE FINANCIAL PERFORMANCE

Sustainability can and should be considered an integral part of shareholder value calculations. Whether a company chooses to contribute to social and environmental improvement is its choice. But the consequences both of doing and of not doing are increasingly being reflected on the bottom line. Physical and social environments are reaching critical thresholds of overcrowding, resource depletion, pollution, climate change, food scarcity, and poverty. The trend toward critical thresholds of sustainability is reflected in higher costs to companies in the following forms:

- Higher materials and energy costs
- Site remediation and cleanup
- Stricter environmental legislation leading to tougher standards of pollution control
- Penalties for exceeding legislated limits
- Consumer disaffection for a company they consider harmful to the environment, sometimes called the *polluter discount*
- Investor disaffection for a company deemed harmful to the environment

- Higher cost of credit as banks look at environmental performance of borrowers
- Degraded markets resulting from social misery, poverty, and violence

The World Business Council for Sustainable Development analyzed the relation between environmental performance and stock market performance. The council found that although this relationship is historically weak, "a growing body of work suggests that companies which rate highly on environmental criteria also provide better-than-average returns to shareholders."[2] The report cited the performance of investment funds, such as Scudder, Stevens & Clark, that invest in companies worldwide that rank among the top in environmental performance within their industry sectors. In the case of Scudder, Stevens & Clark, the fund ranks in the top twentieth percentile among global equity funds. Other studies, such as one by ICF Kaiser, suggest that green strategies might lead to substantial reduction in the perceived risk of a company. Part of the reason is that good environmental management is increasingly taken as an indicator of the overall quality of a company's management. Evidence also exists to support the conclusion that companies with the worst environmental performance score lower than average in stock market returns.[3]

A carefully articulated environmental policy is sound business judgment. However, it necessitates working back from the future rather than extrapolating the past. The discontinuities we face in social and environmental degradation are not likely to be linear projections of past trends. Air quality will not worsen just a little. Water scarcity will affect much more than garden sprinkling. Soil erosion will soon bring entire populations to the brink of starvation. Climatic change involving more than a few degrees of temperature is expected to be violent. Poverty and violence can trigger widespread breakdown in the seamless global economy. Unfortunately, the time horizon on many of these events is shortening. Managers familiar with discounting cash flow will know that as the event horizon approaches, its potential financial impact grows. It no longer makes business sense to ignore impending social and environmental thresholds.

THE SHIFT IN ENVIRONMENTAL RESPONSIBILITY FROM GOVERNMENT TO BIG BUSINESS

Companies today have unprecedented power to set standards in their industries. Market leaders help determine which products and services are offered, how they are manufactured, how by-products are disposed of, which communities will benefit from their investments, and which will not. The power to influence future consumer behavior and even quality-of-life issues has led to a growing public awareness of corporate responsibility for the physical and social environment. Companies with irresponsible industry, community, or ecological practices are quickly identified and punished by government regulation, consumer disaffection, community outcry, and in some cases criminal charges. Past examples have included Exxon, Union Carbide, Philip Morris, and Sandoz. In contrast, companies that pursue green strategies and socially responsible employment and investment policies are enjoying a host of benefits that range from less government interference to increased sales and higher stock-market valuations. Companies such as The Body Shop, Ben & Jerry's, Weyerhauser, Monsanto, Novo Nordisk, Nestle, F. Hoffmann–La Roche, and DuPont have made environmental sustainability a key to differentiating themselves from competitors.

Such power and influence in social and environmental policy are a relatively new industry phenomenon. Consider, for example, Rachel Carson's best-selling *Silent Spring*, published in 1962. One of the seminal books of the ecological movement, it was a remarkable even if highly controversial synthesis of scientific investigation and journalistic reporting. It documented the damage to the environment from indiscriminate spraying of DDT, aldrin, heptachlor, dieldrin, and other pesticides and chemicals in use between the 1920s and the 1950s in the United States and Europe. The dramatic reductions in bird populations, the virtual disappearance of foxes, raccoons, and other small wild animals, and the sudden deaths of large numbers of domesticated animals were ascribed to the use of these chemicals with willful ignorance of their true toxicity. Several documented cases of human exposure and subsequent disease and death were documented. The book emphasized the interdependence of ecological systems and sharply contrasted it with the prevailing view that local effects and habitats were independent of one another and therefore could be isolated.

What is most striking to a reader of *Silent Spring* nearly forty years after its publication is the almost complete attribution of responsibility to government. The Department of Agriculture, the House of Commons, and the World Health Organization are the villains in the story. Only the briefest mention is made of business enterprise—an oblique reference to cases of cancer, lung disease, and liver poisoning among industrial workers.[4] Clearly in Rachel Carson's world of the early 1960s, ecological stress was the responsibility and a problem of government not of business.

In the world of the year 2000, the primary focus for ecological stress and remediation has shifted away from governments and international organizations. Government still plays a fundamental role in setting standards for pollution control, in defining wastes, and in enforcing compliance. The Environmental Protection Agency and individual state authorities assume this responsibility in the United States; in Europe it is ministries of the environment; in other countries it is the ministry of the interior. The United Nations also plays a role through the United Nations Industrial Development Organization (UNIDO), the United Nations Education Science and Culture Organization (UNESCO), the United Nations Institute for Training and Research (UNITAR), and the United Nations Development Programme (UNDP) as do meetings of heads of states such as the earth summit in Rio de Janeiro in 1992 and the Kyoto conference on global warming in 1997.

The villains of this story are now primarily business enterprises, and increasingly the burden for easing ecological stress is being shared between governments and private industry. The concept of industrial enterprise as villain gained momentum in the last two decades of the twentieth century. Writing thirty years after Rachel Carlson, Paul Hawken eloquently made the case for business as the primary source of environmental degradation and sustainability.[5] The ecological disasters of the last fifteen years, with the exception of Chernobyl, were the result of private enterprise. The list includes Union Carbide's pesticide plant explosion in Bhopal, India; the *Exxon Valdez* oil spill off the coast of Alaska; and the Sandoz spill into the Rhine. At the industry level, ecological stress has now come to include the following:

- The link between the hole in the ozone layer and the manufacture of chloroflurocarbons by chemical giants
- The deforestation of Brazil by mining and lumber companies
- The depletion of many of the world's renewable resources, including soil, water, and fisheries
- The disappearance of entire local ecologies, the earliest example being Lake Erie
- The link between global warming and sulfur, carbon monoxide, and carbon dioxide pollution by smokestack industries
- The production of solid industrial wastes in the form of slag, acid, ash, and other by-products of manufacturing processes that now are being ponded or landfilled in waste dumps

Companies are increasingly held accountable for their contributions to the health and prosperity of local communities. The decision of a large multinational company to close a manufacturing or assembly plant employing several thousand workers can spell disaster for a township in terms of employment and income, tax revenue, infrastructure, social investment in education, and social problems such as homelessness. The way in which plants are closed is increasingly coming under the spotlight. Did the company seek other solutions first? Was outplacement assistance provided? What terms did the company offer those who could not find employment?

FIVE TRENDS THAT ENSURE ENVIRONMENTAL DRIVERS ARE HERE TO STAY

A distinct shift has occurred in the political and economic awareness of ecological and social issues. The 1992 Rio earth summit was the first acknowledgment of the pivotal role of business in providing solutions to environmental problems. A greater number of sensitive interfaces now exist between companies and the environment. Small and seemingly external events that concern local operations (for example, site cleanup) can balloon into major business issues for a global company and have direct profit-and-loss consequences.

The following five trends confirm and augment the business effect of social and ecological strategies. Environmental sustainability as a business issue is here to stay and will influence companies in a growing number of industries, whether they are willing participants or not.

Population Growth

Population growth is imposing a burden on the physical resources of the planet, which cannot be sustained with current political and economic institutions. Consumerism has spread to almost all countries, bringing material benefits but also social and ecological stress. Urban overcrowding, pollution, disease, poverty, and migration are spilling over national borders and reducing the effectiveness of governments and other national institutions. The end of the cold war facilitated this spread of unbridled capitalism and the domination of the private corporation as the primary institution of economic activity. With six billion people on earth, early signs of breakdown in global ecologies and shortages in basic needs are already showing. What will it be like when earth supports twice the current population, or even four times current levels, as some demographers suggest will be the case by 2050?

Industrial Consolidation

Industrial consolidation has meant substantial world market shares for the top four or five players in industries ranging from chemicals and cement to telecommunication and computer software. This allows a handful of companies in each industry to set standards and influence industry practices in areas such as product technology, product use, pollution levels, and employment conditions.

Information Technology

Information technology makes it possible for consumers, competitors, and regulators to know instantly how a company exercises its corporate responsibility. The case of Nike, accused by labor and human rights activists of running sweatshops in China and Indonesia and of abusing female workers who make sneakers in Vietnam, is an illustration of the new sensitivities to corporate ethics. The negative business effect occurred despite evidence collected by former Atlanta mayor Andrew Young, hired by Nike to clear its name, that Nike's practices were mainly responsible and ethical.

The Pace of Change

The increasing pace of change has brought the consequences of long-term policies and actions into the short-term. A deteriorating physical environment, increasingly impoverished consumers, negative news coverage, and social anomie can affect a business within very short periods of time. The speed of divergence between successful growth economies and stagnating or chaotic ones in eastern Europe is an example of how fundamental changes in an entire geographic region can occur in just a few years. By the late 1990s from what seemed to be a relatively undifferentiated zone of former Soviet satellite states emerged Poland, the Czech Republic, Slovakia, Slovenia, and Hungary as star performers, whereas Bulgaria, Moldavia, Romania, and the former Yugoslavia languished with little or no investment.

Changing Value Systems

The hallmark of changing value systems is a grassroots sociological movement toward greater spirituality, self-expression, ecological sustainability, and social conscience. On the basis of an extensive survey in the United States in 1995, Paul H. Ray, vice-president of American LIVES Inc., estimated that forty-four million people, about one fourth of the U.S. adult population, were actively adopting these values. "Cultural creatives," as Ray called them, tend to be middle to upper class and statistically represent a forty to sixty male to female ratio.

REVISITING THE CASH FLOW STATEMENT: ENVIRONMENTAL SUSTAINABILITY QUANTIFIED

A clear need exists in most companies to translate environmental drivers into financial information. It used to be that "the business of business is business" meant that environmental issues were considered extraneous to the goals and obligations of companies. After all, governments exist to regulate industry practice as well as to apply laws regarding what is permissible for companies in terms of employment, pollution, technology, competition, shareholder responsibility, and the like. As long as the law is respected, consumers should be free to choose which products and services they want, and companies should be free to supply them. As a result of this kind of thinking, the strategy, organization, and financial reporting structures of most companies are not set up to identify, prioritize, and use environmental drivers for value creation. In this section we propose financial items that can help managers quantify environmental impact.

Before applying quantitative analyses of environmental impact, companies have to ask themselves whether their strategy and organization explicitly deal with these issues. Does the company have an environmental policy? Does implementation of the policy fall into line responsibility? What environmental certification systems exist (EMAS, ISO-14001)? Does a budget exist for environmental assessment and product development? Without a company-wide framework for dealing with environmental policy, attempts to translate environmental drivers into financial information will remain a piecemeal effort with relatively low likelihood for implementation.

MODIFICATION OF CASH FLOW ACCOUNTS FOR SUSTAINABILITY

The following are a number of cash flow accounts that are additions to existing profit-and-loss, working capital, and investment tables. The list is not comprehensive, and it is not applicable in all cases. Shrewd adaptation of these accounts to each company's specific situation is the best approach to quantifying environmental drivers.

- Avoiding negative-impact costs, such as pollution penalties imposed by government for exceeding emission norms or publicity campaigns aimed at cleaning up an image of polluter or sweatshop manufacturer
- Reducing energy consumption costs through designing more efficient plants or using waste-derived fuel sources such as household or industrial refuse

- Reducing materials costs by recycling products that would otherwise end up in landfills or by using scrap from industries in which materials can be economically recovered
- Increasing volume by offering consumers products perceived to be environmentally friendly or by distinguishing a brand based on green economics
- Introducing price premiums based on the perception that a product is environmentally friendly or based on a corporate image of social and environmental responsibility
- Lowering costs of credit, either from international financial institutions such as the World Bank or IBRD (International Bank for Reconstruction and Development) or from private-sector banks, which increasingly offer lower loan rates to companies that can prove environmental performance
- Developing new business by providing environmental solutions to the nonsustainable activities of other businesses

Box 16.1 Volvo Trucks

In the 1990s, Volvo introduced the FH truck series with a new D12 engine with considerably lower fuel consumption and emission levels than other models. Volvo publicized extensively the environmental benefits of the new trucks as a point of differentiation from the competition. Since the introduction of the FH series, Volvo has increased market share of over-sixteen-ton trucks by thirty-five percent in Europe, nearly doubled operating margins relative to its ten-year average, and raised the truck division's share of operating income from thirty to fifty-six percent.

The cash costs and benefits of sustainable strategies have to be explicitly built into pro forma strategic plans, investment proposals, and annual budgets. Solid shareholder value analysis will ensure that unprofitable sustainable strategies are avoided and that profitable ones will have the full support of management.

In the 1980s and 1990s, companies discovered the costs of poorly engineered business processes. Being in the right business and carrying out the right activities is no longer enough, even when excellent management teams are involved. As Peter Keen has argued,[6] a key to value creation has become investing and maintaining core *processes*, whether these be product development, procurement, delivery, or any other value-generating activity that differentiates a company from its competitors. Each process has a cost measured in acquisition of know-how and experience. Many companies leave this cost out of their cash flow calculations.

A parallel exists for valuing sustainable strategies. The social and environmental actions undertaken by companies have direct cash flow consequences, whether the companies like it or not and whether these actions are the result of intended decisions or the by-products of short-term profit motives. Management ethics has immediate implications for the bottom line, and this relation will continue to grow as global and local ecological and social problems become more accentuated.

WHAT IS AT STAKE: OUR PLANET

There are about six billion people in the world today. Twenty-five percent or 1.5 billion live below the poverty line in what is being called the subsistence economy. These people live day to day in search of food, shelter, and firewood and have no margin for responsible social and environmental behavior. Current projections put the world population at more than twelve billion persons by 2030. The earth is already badly stressed in terms of depletion of natural resources, air and water pollution, soil erosion, deforestation, overfishing, and decreased habitable space. What will a doubling of the world's population bring? What will happen to planetary stress if the developing countries with three fourths of the world's population try to live western lifestyles?

The answer is, we don't know. Planetary limits are not solid walls against which we crash unless we come to a timely stop. They are thresholds beyond which breakdown and chaos are probable but not certain. Chaos theory provides ample evidence that very complex systems do not bear stress in a linear manner. Small instabilities can be absorbed by the system up to a critical point; then discontinuities appear. But this is only theory.

Taken on a case-by-case basis, the evidence of impending disaster is insufficient to mobilize a mainstream reaction. In the developed world, each of us continues to live a lifestyle that will consume over an expected life, eight hundred thousand kilowatts of electrical energy, two hundred fifty million liters of water, twenty-one thousand liters of gasoline, two hundred twenty kilograms of steel, and the wood of one thousand trees. There is no compelling reason to give up the things we currently enjoy, even if these things cannot last. Our children's generation will have to consume a little less, or perhaps they will find solutions to planetary stress that we cannot yet imagine.

Growing evidence exists that we are pushing environmental and social limits beyond sustainable levels with perhaps dramatic consequences. Continued greenhouse emissions, particularly carbon dioxide, could lead to small temperature changes that would have catastrophic consequences for low-lying countries and for the world's weather patterns. Continued consumption of fresh water at greater than renewal rates will cause serious water shortages, particularly in North Africa, the Middle East, India, and central Asia. Continued overfishing could deplete the stocks supplying basic food to large segments of the world population. Continued

soil erosion will make it impossible for subsistence populations to nourish themselves on even the most basic foods such
as rice and sorghum.

In all, about seven billion tons of carbon dioxide is
pumped into the atmosphere each year. An estimated seventy
thousand chemical compounds are discharged into air, soil,
and water. The World Bank estimates that by 2010 there will
be more than a billion motor vehicles in the world. If existing
automobile technology continues, these cars will double
current levels of energy use, smog precursors, and emissions
of greenhouse gases. Industrial wastes estimated at two
hundred million tons are dumped into the oceans annually.
Although power-generating plants, government pesticide
programs, sewage sludge, nuclear weapons disposal sites,
and other public sector polluting activities continue to contribute heavily to environmental damage, manufacturing
industries in the private sector bear a primary responsibility
for these statistics.

Even partial continuation of these nonsustainable practices might lead to mass migrations, communication break-
downs, resource shortages, civil wars, and environmental
degradation on an unimaginable scale. At best, it will mean
preservation of a few islands of privilege in a sea of poverty
and violence. The nature of the damage is transforming itself
from local and containable to global and life threatening.
Examples of global and life-threatening environmental
damage are global warming, ozone depletion, loss of tropical
forests, and contamination of food and drinking water in
broad rural and urban areas. Each type of damage has the
potential to disrupt life on our planet as we know it.

Global companies cannot be expected to be the sole
participants in the planetary survival dance. Changes in
lifestyles and expectations of individuals will be paramount.
Governments and multilateral organizations must raise and
enforce sustainability targets. We recognize, however, that
leading companies often are the only organizations with the
resources, the technology, the local presence, the global reach,

and ultimately the motivation to restore and sustain the physical and social environments in which they operate. In the following section we examine the opportunities and sources of value creation that exist for companies in search of sustainability strategies.

OPPORTUNITIES AND SOURCES OF VALUE CREATION

Globalism, ecological sustainability, spirituality, a growing planetary conscience, and social optimism are part of a broadbased grass roots sociological movement. This shift in values and a shift in attribution of responsibility are creating a new dimension in the corporate environment. In effect, the sociological expectations of ecological sustainability are translating themselves into economic forces of supply and demand.

Opportunities and sources of value creation for companies exist in several distinct forms. The first is penalty avoidance, which consists mostly of piecemeal projects designed to control pollution or social costs within the limits of the law. The second is elimination of nonsustainable practices in production processes through minimization or elimination of waste or by-products that necessitate costly remediation. The third source of opportunity and value creation is product life-cycle sustainability through recovery, recycling, and reuse. The fourth is development of products and services that purposely contribute environmental solutions to existing problems. Each of these sources of opportunity and value creation is looked at in turn.[7]

Penalty Avoidance

Most companies are still operating at the penalty-avoidance level. The pressure is to comply with legislation on air, land, and water pollution limits. This is primarily a penal interface. Lack of compliance leads to fines, loss of permits, lawsuits, and in some cases, prison sentences for individual managers.

Consider Hilados y Tejidos Puignero SA, a Spanish textile company found guilty of illegal dumping chemical dyes and detergents into local rivers. In 1997, the company's owner, J. Puignero, was sentenced to four years in prison and fined nearly $50,000 in addition to $170,000 of assessed penalties.[8]

In other cases, companies have been penalized for individual accidents (the *Exxon Valdez* incident), for unfair social practices real or imagined (Nike's alleged use of Asian sweatshops), and for selling products harmful to the public health (Philip Morris). In still other cases, companies willingly bear the costs of site remediation and pollution cleanup to operate a profitable but polluting technology. In general, companies today have accepted their responsibility to respect the law and adhere to industry standards related to pollution levels, safety, and social practices.

Eliminating Nonsustainable Practices in Production Processes

Redesigned manufacturing processes can prevent pollution. New technologies can eliminate the use of toxic materials or by-products. When giant chemical companies such as BASF began colocating facilities in which the waste from one process became the raw material for another, a source of waste was eliminated and a source of energy was conserved. Paint producers have largely switched from solvent-phased to water-phased production. Cement companies burn waste fuels derived from the manufacturing processes of other companies in a win-win situation of lower costs and less pollution. Concrete producers substitute fly ash, a by-product of coal-burning power plants that otherwise must be landfilled or ponded, for cement in their mixing trucks with no decrease in product performance.

Danish Steel Works, under attack from the Danish environmental protection agency in high-cost northern Europe, converted an environmental threat into a business opportunity by using scrap instead of high-grade iron ore and by improving resource productivity, a savings that goes directly to the bottom line. The possibilities are endless for such creative redesign of manufacturing processes. Because many existing production systems are the fruits of research and development undertaken before environmental and social issues came to the fore, there is true potential for improvement.

Product Life-Cycle Sustainability

When Dunlop Tire Corporation and Akzo Nobel developed, in the mid 1990s, a new radial tire that had an aramid fiber belt rather than the conventional steel belt, they helped the environment through lower recycling costs and helped consumers with improved safety and gas mileage. DuPont's agricultural products division developed a new herbicide that is effective at one to five percent of the application rates of traditional chemicals, is nontoxic to animals and nontargeted species of plants, biodegrades in the soil, and leaves virtually no residue on crops. Because it requires much less material in its manufacture, the new chemical also is highly profitable.

Hartmann, a publicly traded packaging and paper company, uses exclusively recycled paper and meets all customer requirements for texture and whiteness. Additional financial value comes from matching competitor product performance and adding another critical dimension the competition cannot meet. For industrial customers, who themselves are under market pressure to show environmentally responsible performance, the Hartmann green guarantee is increasingly valuable.

To ensure life-cycle sustainability all of the effects that a product might have on the environment are examined during the design phase. Such cradle-to-grave analysis starts and ends outside the traditional boundaries of a company's operations. It includes assessing the environmental impact of the raw materials and services purchased in the manufacturing process and evaluating the use and disposal of the product.

Environmental Solutions to Existing Problems

Aeroquip Corporation, a $2.5 billion manufacturer of hoses, fittings, and couplings, was able to generate $250 million in business within six years by focusing on the waste reduction and pollution control of other companies. Before entering this new field, Aeroquip had never thought about sustainability or providing environmental solutions to the emission control problems of others. Yet it was able to translate an opportunity based on a fit with existing product technology into a profitable proenvironment business. Monsanto's genetic engineering of plants that eliminates altogether the need for pesticides is another example of sustainability strategies focused on environmental solutions to existing problems. So are examples of socially responsible investing such as the American Express commitment to the World Monuments Fund or Grand Metropolitan's community involvement described in its report on corporate citizenship.

Kvaerner, one of the world's largest engineering companies, is a leading manufacturer of systems and technologies for the environmentally friendly solutions needed in processing natural resources such as forests, oil, natural gas, minerals, steel, and hydropower. It introduced the EcoPlus performance program, which involved setting quantified goals in energy productivity, environmentally friendly technology such as chlorine-free paper pulp manufacturing, reduced insurance costs, and improved health and safety. In each area, Kvaerner expects substantial savings or increased profits. Financial analysts agree. According to a recent securities report, "a very favorable risk-reward ratio makes Kvaerner the only blue chip on the Oslo Stock Exchange that may double its value over the next twelve months."[9]

In other cases of environmental stewardship, special foundations are established, for example, the Rhine Foundation created by Sandoz in part to remedy the disaster it caused. In still other cases, companies sponsor ecological conservation acts, such as Elf's *radeau des cimes* effort to control rain forest destruction in central Africa. Companies hope to cash in on perceived stakeholder value, which includes increased sales, increased stock valuation, and less government regulation.

Box 16.2 Environmental Action at Lafarge

"Caring for the Environment is an essential element of the Group's long-term strategy." So begins Lafarge's environmental policy report, signed by chairman and chief executive officer Bertrand Collomb. As a cement producer and manufacturer of a range of production materials from ready-mix concrete to specialty chemicals, Lafarge is in the forefront of environmentally sensitive industrial activity. As the world leader in construction materials and present in more than forty-five countries, Lafarge has a special responsibility for setting industry standards and norms of conduct.

Under Collomb's leadership, Lafarge has gone farther than just respecting local laws and regulations when it comes to emissions and the impact of its operations on the environment and communities in which it operates. Lafarge's environmental initiatives are aimed at shaping future national regulatory requirements, for example in emerging markets such as those of the former Soviet Union and China. Its research and development program is aimed at innovating products that provide comfort, health, and aesthetics while integrating life-cycle effects on the environment (mining, manufacturing, distribution, use, and disposal).

Explicit environmental sustainability programs at Lafarge include the following:

• Reducing fuel consumption and carbon dioxide emissions

- Switching sources to waste-derived fuels
- Substituting by-products for natural sources of aluminum, iron, and gypsum in cement production
- Reusing fly ash, slag, and silica fume in ready-mix concrete production through mix designs that simultaneously improve concrete performance and lower costs to consumers
- Reusing desulfogypse rather than natural gypsum in wallboard production
- Recultivating quarries and industrial sites
- Recycling concrete and gypsum waste on job sites
- Innovating environmentally friendly products such as gypsum drywall that is fire resistant, thermally insulating, and acoustically dampening
- Designing efficient plants

Lafarge is studying economical solutions to recycling materials derived from demolished building sites. The concept of a recycled building presents numerous difficulties because of the presence of nonmineral materials such as plastic, iron, and wood, but in large cities where natural materials may have to be transported from a great distance, the promise of recycling centers exists.

The results are significant: in key markets, Lafarge has already achieved a fifty percent decrease in energy consumption per ton of cement, forty-five percent waste-derived fuel substitution in individual cement plants, seventeen percent substitution of by-product gypsum for natural gypsum, and increasing substitution of fly ash and slag for natural cement.

The social consequences of global business decisions are becoming more visible, offering greater opportunities for differentiation but greater potential costs. Consider, for example, the fate of several local communities caught in the crosswinds of global corporations in the mid 1990s. The decision by French car maker Renault SA to close its plant in the Brussels suburb of Vilvoorde will deal a devastating blow to the battered industrial town, where angry citizens demonstrated in the streets and considered litigation alternatives. Also consider British Petroleum's decision to shut down its oil refinery plant in Lima, Ohio. The decision came despite thirty percent improvement in productivity and despite interest from other petroleum companies in buying the plant, including Ashland Oil Inc. and Solar Refining Corp. Lima's mayor, David Berger, accused BP of deliberately making sure that the plant was destroyed so that no competitor could reuse it. BP's decision made the front page of the *Wall Street Journal*, in a feature article titled "American Town Feels the Blow of Decisions Made an Ocean Away: BP's Closing of Ohio Refinery Shows Downside of Distant Bosses—Should Firms Pay 'Social Rent'?"[10]

Ecological and social interdependence is a systems-creating force for a corporation. It obliges the corporation to think and act in a holistic and dynamic sense about its environment, rather than in the conventional static and reductionistic way possible with customers, competitors, and suppliers. There are other systems-creating drivers outside its immediate competitive environment, notably interactions between the corporation and society in the domains of culture, education, sports, and politics. These interactions have always existed, but as in the linkage to ecology and local communities, it is only in recent years, and in combination with the factors of globalization and information technology and diffusion, that a new set of dynamics have arisen.

For a growing number of companies, perpetual transformation has come to include environmental sustainability as a key element of shareholder value. It will be up to creative and foresighted managers in these companies to apply and extend this broader approach to their own specific cases. In doing so they will have the opportunity to turn responsible environmental management into a profitable and sustainable future for themselves, their companies, and the world in which they live and work.

Chapter 17

Conclusion

The chief executive officers of Fortune 500 companies often are larger than life in the breadth of their vision and in their ability to intuitively get it right when it comes to steering large organizations into an uncertain future. In the ranks below these leaders, however, are senior and middle managers who are confronted with a difficult challenge. They possess fine technical skills, operating experience, and sharp minds, but they can't seem to unlock the secrets to transforming their organizations. In turbulent competitive environments, these middle and upper managers often resist change or at best become passive bystanders. They find a host of reasons why not to do things differently from in the past and in the process become less effective, and more frustrated, in their jobs.

Perpetual transformation, embodied by the Ten Principles, offers managers insight into this difficult challenge of leadership in large organizations. Each manager and business unit has a unique challenge to effective transformation, whether driven by emerging technologies, global market forces, changing consumer expectations, tougher governmental constraints, or internal leadership problems. The underlying system dynamics of transformation, however, are the same for all. These are the dynamics of complex adaptive systems. They are concerned with a type of change that involves organizational reinvention rather than growth by replication, discontinuity rather than incrementalism, and true innovation rather than a periodic reordering. The Ten Principles offer guidelines to managing in light rather than in ignorance of these dynamics.

Achieving an understanding of the new leadership approach is not an easy quest. It is a challenge that cannot be taken on in a single day or tackled only with conventional analytic tools. Consider how this challenge differs from the more conventional task of formulating a business-unit strategy. A business strategy may require months of data collection and analysis. However, it can be conveyed in a matter of hours. A project leader recommends an action (build a new plant in market A) based on a set of issues (improve cost competitiveness) and data collected (customer interviews and recent competitor investments). Senior management either agrees with the conclusions and recommendations or it does not. If management agrees, the project is likely to be approved, and implementation begins. In this process, the strategic formulation is *transferred* to senior management in a brief moment in time through the power of analysis and persuasion.

Perpetual transformation is not an analytic or consensual exercise in decision making. It requires a new view of reality based on the emerging vision from the sciences of complexity, chaos, and evolution. The distinctions and insights contained in this book must be grasped progressively and built into new managerial reflexes. They must be understood as parts of a new managerial outlook. Any one principle taken in isolation will appear confusing or without meaning to a career manager who has never thought in these terms.

Like Thomas Mann, writing in the postscript to his extraordinarily perceptive novel *The Magic Mountain*, we wish that our readers could read our book not once but twice to achieve a more complete understanding. Better yet, we wish our readers the courage to live the Ten Principles on the job, even if it means risking the present for a powerful future. The game we play is about achieving extraordinary business results and boosting shareholder value. It also is about personal success. In this sense, our approach has similar objectives to more traditional management concerns with value-chain economics, customer segmentation, product innovation, time-based competition, and the like. Rather than seeking to replace conventional approaches, it attempts to make them more effective. Perpetual transformation is an additional knowledge base with which to equip practicing managers faced with steering large organizations in hurricane seas of change.

Appendix 1

The New Corporate Reality

In this appendix we describe the complexity, turbulence, and contradictions faced by companies in today's competitive environment. Our observations are drawn from a careful review of changes in the world economy and from everyday life inside multinational companies. We review the twin motors of the new corporate reality: the trend toward globality and the ongoing information revolution. In light of the new corporate reality, we invite the reader to rethink what is a global corporation. The key features are quite different from those that appear, often implicitly, in traditional management thinking. These key features help us to reenvision the corporate world in which many of us live and work.

Not so long ago, companies enjoyed protected prosperity for extended periods during which they focused on growth by means of replication (producing more of the same product with the same technology) rather than growth by means of transformation. Not only Ford with its famous example of a Model T car produced only in black but also IBM, Procter & Gamble, Sears, Citibank, Aetna, and hundreds of other leading companies counted on the fact that tomorrow would look like today. Business catastrophes happened as they have throughout history, but the pace and amplitude of change allowed for long-term forecasting and planning. When major change occurred, it was often caused by war, disease, famine, or the politics of a new government. The key features of industry—the products, production methods, trading routes, markets, merchant families, and bankers—remained remarkably stable over long periods. Extended periods of little change punctuated by occasional disasters have existed since at least the twelfth century *corps de métiers* (from which the word *corporation* is derived) in France, if not since the Venetian maritime trading firms (*societas maris*) of the ninth and tenth centuries.[1]

Since the 1970s, the pace and amplitude of change have increased to the point of *continuous discontinuity*. A new competitive landscape is emerging, the hallmarks of which are complexity and rapid, turbulent change. Tomorrow is no longer anything like today, and we are regularly confronted with complete uncertainty by new competitors, new technologies, new consumer expectations, new regulations, and new products and services. The level of complexity, measured in the raw amount of information necessary to do business over any given period of time, is growing exponentially. Consider the following cases of unexpected and unpredictable change over periods of time ranging from several months to a few years:

- Internet start-up companies, such as Amazon.com, eBay, and E-Trade, and Web-based assemblers such as Monorail, have taken explosive market share at the expense of traditional competitors. Manufacturers also are finding competitive advantage in shifting operations to the Web. Witness the success of communication equipment maker Cisco.

- After a century of French-only competition, the regional unit of Lafarge cements in Normandy finds itself suddenly competing against low-cost Greek importers with delivered prices under production costs. This event was brought on by the availability of low-cost international shipping by which bulk cement can be transported halfway across the world for a fraction of production costs.

• BP's decision to shut down an oil refinery in Lima, Ohio, creates a disaster for the town, as did Daimler-Benz AG's decision to pull the funding plug on NV Fokker in the Dutch town of Papendrecht.

In each case, the marketplace was suddenly made more complex with new competitors, new sources of competitive advantage, new costs, and new regulatory constraints. Such events are difficult to predict, difficult to control, and very fast to snowball into disaster or success or disappear entirely.

The contradictions, paradoxes, and soft factors present in the new corporate reality are a direct outgrowth of faster change and greater complexity in the everyday work environment. The new reality is also of considerable discomfort to most managers, some of whom began their careers in the 1950s and 1960s, when corporate stability, unambiguous hierarchical structure, predictable change, and hard facts and analyses ruled the day.

Traditional managerial culture emphasizes measurement and control. It favors unambiguous organizational structures and values predictability and stability. The quantitative methods used in business school curricula and in engineering programs rely heavily on quantitative methods. The major management processes themselves are essentially cartesian in approach. They are rational and reductionistic and based on a cause-and-effect model of reality. Annual budgets, investment pro forma worksheets, accounting statements, strategic plans, and statistical analyses all are used to bolster the credibility of management decisions by means of bringing hard facts and rigorous analyses to support fully controllable conclusions and recommendations.

The value placed on forecasting by the chief executive officer of a large U.S. company captures this search for determinism and control: "I believe if you can predict your numbers correctly, you have a firm understanding of where they're coming from. You know cause and effect. And once you know cause and effect, you can control it. We want people to think, 'I'm in control. I *know* what I need to do to make that number different.' "[2]

Determinism and control are increasingly at odds with the uncertainty and incongruities faced on a daily basis by managers in large organizations. Consider the following pervasive corporate-life contradictions to what we are taught to expect and value:

• Leaders are required to be more charismatic and competent than ever, yet they are expected to empower their people by delegating decision making and decentralizing ever more. Increased power and responsibility often mean less control and fewer opportunities to use hands-on competencies. Interviewed in the *Harvard Business Review* about how he infuses new thinking into his employees, Robert Shapiro, chief executive officer of the chemicals giant Monsanto, said, "Its not hard. You talk for three minutes, and people light up and say, 'Where do we start?' And I say, 'I don't know. And good luck.' "[3]

• Companies are expected to maintain a fixed, long-term identity and image, yet competitive pressures often force them to reposition their core business on a continual basis. Insurance companies subcontract data processing and enter the fields of health care or automobile repair. Ford earns more money in some years from consumer financing than from car sales. British Airways has become a major player in the hotel reservations business. Through all these transformations, the companies' various stakeholders expect a steadfast core image and reputation.

• As products and processes become complex, customers demand greater simplicity in dealing with the supplying organization. Providing customers with this simplicity, however, creates ever-greater complexity in the products and processes. Companies such as Macdonald's have made an art of providing seemingly simple products with very complex (and difficult to imitate) processes of procurement, training, and production sequencing.

• Helping direct competitors can improve a company's medium- and long-term profitability. Some industries ignore this paradox through unbridled competitive warfare. Examples are commercial airlines in the 1980s (Pan Am, TWA, Eastern Airlines), retailers (Macy's, Bloomingdale's), and computer companies (Digital, Wang, and Data General). In other industries, such as pharmaceuticals, banking, and telecommunication, the use of signaling, voluntary compliance to industry norms and standards, and alliances and partnerships of various sorts provide the conditions for sustainable, profitable activity for all players.

• Negotiating tougher price conditions with a supplier can be a disadvantage. A story is told of a purchasing agent at Hewlett-Packard who bragged to the chief executive officer about a deal he had just negotiated with a supplier in which he had forced the price down by fifty percent. The chief executive officer questioned whether the supplier could make a fair profit at that price and eventually called in the supplier to renegotiate a fairer price. Hewlett-Packard thereby gained a loyal supplier for life.

• Some companies have great people, great products, a great strategy, and a sizable war chest but cannot implement anything. This was IBM in the 1970s. It had a world-class marketing organization, outstanding product development, and an ability to attract the very best people. Yet the company almost did not survive the next fifteen years. Over time, these companies lose market share, underperform their industry and eventually restructure under crisis conditions or disappear.

• Great accomplishments provide short-lived benefits. Individual or company achievements rarely reap long-term rewards of recognition, job security, and financial compensation, because they are quickly imitated or over-taken.

• As instability increases, managers with more stable and dependable styles are often favored by their organizations. The qualities of persistence and doggedness are prized in volatile and fast-changing environments.

The underlying conditions that give rise to the contradictions and paradoxes of managerial life are here to stay. We are not in the midst of a short-lived period of turbulence about to return to a golden epoch of stability and simplicity. As Charles Handy wrote in *The Age of Paradox* "[Managers] can, and should, reduce the starkness of some of the contradictions, minimize the inconsistencies, understand the puzzles in the paradox, but [they] cannot make them disappear, solve them completely, or escape from them."[4] Perpetual transformation is about working with this reality.

The twin motors of globalization and informatization underlie the phenomenal rise in complexity and its attendant contradictions in management. *Globalization* is a widely used term that covers a multitude of separate innovations, market extensions, converging consumer values, and political developments. We review the advent of globalization because it is the primary aspect of the new corporate reality for all companies no matter what their products, services, markets, or geographic scope. The Lafarge regional sales unit in Normandy is a good example of a business that had always considered itself local and protected (conventional wisdom had it that cement is a low-value product that competes only in the local market in which it is produced) but suddenly faced exchange-rate variations and structurally lower production costs from distant competitors. Even the most archetypal local businesses are now part of the global game.

GLOBALIZATION

The extent of the globalization of business since the Second World War and of the growth of its share of economic power is remarkable but seldom fully appreciated. The confluence of production, commerce, the technologies of information and control, and the stable political scene provided business with the opportunity and the means to span the world. In search of profits and competitive advantage an increasing number of enterprises went national, then multinational, and then global.

In the immediately postwar years U.S. corporations in search of profits pioneered the shift from the national to the international level. The driver was the low cost of labor overseas. In the process these corporations transferred considerable know-how and technology to the host countries. Competitive domestic industries arose in Europe, Asia, and Latin America. Before long, some of the overseas companies, especially in Japan, caught up with and even surpassed their U.S. counterparts in competitiveness, profitability, and market share. While U.S. companies were still seeking cheap labor off shore, the Japanese were investing in global market shares using low discount rates to build low-cost positions based on economies of scale. In the automobile industry, for example, the doubling of cumulative production in the manufacture of combustion engines led to a twenty percent reduction in direct unit costs. Large-scale production brought premiums in both quality and price. Expanding into more and more related product branches, Japanese manufacturers such as Honda, Nissan, and Toyota became world industry leaders.

The Americans, with their propensity for gigantism, fought valiantly with the new Asian competition through large-scale investments to build ever-larger operations—the largest factories, the longest runs, the heaviest marketing campaigns, the strongest sales forces. At the same time the Americans were learning to exploit economies (of scale, experience, and technology), the Japanese turned to flexible manufacturing systems, total customer responsiveness, total quality control, constant differentiation, automation, and other systems that helped them become number one in meeting customer demands quickly and at low cost. This latter wave of competitive offense from the Japanese amounted to an increased ability to handle diverse customer and geographic portfolios and therefore increased new product introductions, product range, and manufacturing processes for the same set of resources. Japanese firms learned to better handle more customers in more markets. This also contributed to the internationalization of industry.

With the end of the cold war and the leaner and meaner U.S. economy of the 1990s, the American model of unbridled capitalism stands unchallenged while European social democrats struggle with high unemployment and low rates of growth of the gross domestic product. The American model is increasingly emulated and exported to more and more countries in eastern Europe, Africa, and Asia. Global financial markets have emerged with little or no institutional oversight, and national equity markets stand to rise and fall together.

INFORMATION FLOW

Worldwide flow of information is another driver of the globalization process. Because information can spread rapidly from company to company, it has become more difficult to build competitive advantage through the commercialization of inventions. In the early part of the twentieth century, research and development of new products led to profitable leadership positions that could be conserved, first through patents and later through famous brands; Ford and Ivory soap are good examples. When the knowledge base of innovation became global and almost instantly accessible, imitation quickly led to dissipation of profits in new projects. French television manufacturers were leaders in the development of top-of-the-line models with soft touch and remote control, coming out with these features well ahead of their Japanese counterparts. But because the Japanese were able to take over this new technology and produce better television sets in a very short period of time, success and payback for the French manufacturers remained low. British technological achievements in antibiotics, radar, the jet engine, and even the computer ended up commercialized by non-British firms. Phillips's pioneering innovations with compact disc technology went largely to the Japanese.

As a result of this shortened invention-imitation-dissipation cycle, many firms have shied away from heavy, risky upstream sources of competitive advantage and have turned to new forms of growth and globalization. Firms have moved farther downstream into consumer and service areas but expanded horizontally through mergers and acquisitions. Government deregulation (notably a relaxation of antitrust enforcement under Reagan and Bush and the reduction of protective industry barriers in the European Single Act) and international tax rate differentials have been other motors of increased size and globalization of corporations.

INDUSTRY CONSOLIDATION

The creation of multinational companies constituted one stage in the growth wave of business. The next stage was the emergence of non-national, that is, genuinely global corporations. The multinational giants of the early part of the century treated foreign operations as distant appendages for the production of goods designed, engineered, sold, or serviced in their home countries. The chain of command in these multinational companies was clearly linked to nationality. But by the early 1990s, genuinely global corporations were emerging in which no national origin held sway in technology, capital, labor, or even senior management.

Of course, whether American, European, or Japanese, not every industry can reap the full benefit of internationalization. Some are inherently local because of service content, diseconomies of scale, or costly geographic product differences. Most industries, however, have been able to benefit at some level of activity, such as research and development, raw material sourcing, service rationalization, and revenue generation.

In industries such as biotechnology, aeroengines, banking, and insurance, the accelerating pace of product innovation favors global players with worldwide access to ideas, technologies, capital, and markets. The share of products less than five years old rose from just over forty percent in 1987 to more than fifty-five percent in the late 1990s. Only global players can afford breakthrough research and development budgets in many fields and the risk-taking necessary to introduce successful new products. Rolls Royce, Pratt & Whitney, Mitsubishi Heavy Industries, MBT, and FIAT Industries were all global players when they founded a joint company in the early 1980s—International Aero Engines—to research and develop a new generation of midthrust turbines. Boeing's acquisition of McDonnell Douglas makes it one of only two large-size commercial aircraft manufacturers worldwide. In many industries, global consolidation is the single most important driver of industry structure. It is widely considered, for example, that the strategic alliance of Spain's Telefonica, British Telecommunications, and MCI in the United States will fundamentally redefine the balance of power between telecommunication suppliers, to the disadvantage of AT&T.

The globalization of industrial enterprises has been accompanied by the globalization of trade and services and paralleled by financial markets operating around the clock and around the world. The exchange market is likely to be the most global of all business sectors with worldwide rates, instantaneous electronic banking and arbitrage, and a daily turnover estimated at approximately $1 trillion.

The globalization of business has gradually been eroding the economic sovereignty of nation-states. National governments do not know how to even consider the global players much less how to regulate them. It is not clear what national obligations are applicable to a global company and what nation controls the technology the company has developed. It is also unclear how the operations of a global company should be accounted for. If a U.S. company makes computer components in Japan and sells them in the United States, should its sales be counted as trade deficit, as are U.S. products made in Japan by Japanese companies?

As companies have grown in size and multicountry experience, they have learned to shape national business climates. This is particularly true where national industries have become highly concentrated. In the United States overall manufacturing concentration, measured in share of aggregate manufacturing assets held by the one hundred largest manufacturing companies, rose from thirty-eight in 1945 to fifty-two percent in 1990. Between 1990 and 1998 mergers and acquisitions rose in terms of annual dollar value of deals to more than $1 trillion.[5] Today it is not unusual to find that four or five companies control eighty percent of a market sector. In Japan, an eighty percent market share is frequently reached by fewer than four companies. In Europe, overall manufacturing concentration has been shown to rise measurably. Since the Single Act white paper in 1985, falling protective barriers have caused European concentration to increase (largely through attrition, although mergers and acquisitions are growing increasingly popular on the continent). An increasing number of industries worldwide are being consolidated to a handful of players. The example of Boeing and Airbus is unusual only in the controversy it briefly generated, not in the trend it illustrates. It is thought that the personal computer industry, which shrank from eight hundred thirty-two to four hundred thirty-five companies in the late 1980s, may be reduced to as few as five long-term winners within a few years.[6]

THE SPAN OF POWER OF GLOBAL CORPORATIONS

The economic and political power acquired by global companies is unprecedented in history. The decisions of corporate executives affect the businesses and markets in which they function and the lives and environments of the people in whose communities the businesses operate. By creating large-scale employment, executives influence the distribution of wealth and create social stability. By bringing value-added products and services to the marketplace, they raise the material standard of living and increasingly define which products and services society consumes. Through highly mobile geographic investments in people and technology, executives transform the fabric of society. They influence lifestyles, employment opportunities, and urban-rural balance and impinge on the very survival of cities and states. Responsible industrial investment policies open new paths of development to entire populations. Myopic decisions press whole economies to the edge of bankruptcy and condemn populations to marginal existence if not downright starvation. By employing risky technologies and insufficient safeguards, enterprises degrade the environment and impair the health of millions. Through joint (or at least coordinated) technological efforts, however, the same companies have the power to repair and improve the earth's ecology.

Hence, DuPont and Nemours or Monsanto in the chemicals industry can heavily influence the availability and application of air-borne pollutants. General Motors, Toyota, and PSA can affect emission levels and road safety standards in their respective continents. Lafarge and Holderbank, world industry leaders in building materials, have already set standards in the use of industrial waste in the safe manufacture of cement, thus conserving fossil fuel and reducing waste landfill requirements. The next biggest motors of increased complexity and turbulence are developments in the field of information technology, information management, and knowledge-based industries. These developments are grouped under the term *informatization*.

INFORMATIZATION

Corporations in the machine age relied on a seemingly unlimited supply of raw materials, energy, and substitutable labor. The aim was to produce mass-manufactured products for mass markets; quantity rather than quality was emphasized. In the machine age, success depended on access to the factors of production, access to markets, and efficient functioning of established processes (production, selling, financing, and administration). External openness to information and internal flow of information mattered little relative to the physical transformation of raw materials into finished product.

After the Second World War increases in the complexity of the corporate environment shifted the basis of successful operation to efficient access and use of information. The facilitating factor was advances in information technology itself.

Although innovations in information processing technologies began in early antiquity—the invention of the number system and the alphabet are perhaps the greatest innovations in history—processes accessible to industry have greatly accelerated in modern times. Although some ancient mechanical contraptions extended human computational power, for example the abacus, calculating machines with built-in programs are a relatively modern phenomenon. In 1642, Blaise Pascal invented an adding machine that may have been the first digital calculator. In 1671, Leibniz invented an instrument that multiplied by means of repeated addition. In 1833, Babbage produced the analytical engine and developed a logistical basis for building genuine computing machines.

About one hundred years ago information-processing technologies really took off. Hollerith succeeded in the automation of the census count at the end of the nineteenth century, and Bell invented the telephone. At around the same time, Hertz developed the principle of wireless communication and pioneered the development of the radio. Konrad Zuse built his Z1, Z2, and Z3 computers in the 1930s, and Eckert, Mauchly, and Goldstein built the cumbersome but already accomplished ENIAC computer in 1946. UNIVAC I, a vast machine with five thousand heat-generating vacuum tubes that covered two hundred twenty square feet and weighed five tons, was developed a few years later. However, the computer was not an information-processing technology available to industry. The computers that did exist were the province of government and university research. UNIVAC I, for example, was used in 1952 to predict the victory of Dwight Eisenhower in the U.S. presidential election; use of the computer made a sensation on national television.

The invention of the computational architecture of digital data processing by mathematician John von Neumann allowed a quantum leap in electronic information processing. Through digitalization, numbers, letters, words, sounds, images, and the measurement of mechanical and electrical instruments could be rapidly and accurately transformed into strings of electronic pulses. Computers that processed digital signals became commercially available in the early 1950s and benefited from the concurrent mass production of transistors for hearing aids and radios. In the 1960s, computers entered the field of production. Computer-integrated manufacturing (CIM) harnessed the new-found power of the digital computer to integrate the different elements of manufacturing, so that the entire process could be operated in a single system. Because of the unique capabilities of computers, this system could be flexibly automated and operated on line in real time.

In the 1970s, the development and implementation of the full capabilities of CIM made slow progress because most companies applied computer technology to the automation of isolated elements of manufacturing. They created "islands of automation" with little integration of the bits and pieces within an adaptively optimizing manufacturing system. By the 1980s the situation was changing. Leading manufacturing enterprises became aware of the competitive advantage of overall automation, optimization, and integration in a total-system process of manufacturing. They began to encompass the technological elements of the manufacturing system—product design, production planning and control, shop-floor automation, and inventory control—and such managerial elements as strategic planning, finance, human resources, and marketing.

In the 1990s, CIM allowed firms to maintain production levels with half as many machines as a decade earlier and physical plants half as large. Direct labor costs fell by as much as seventy-five percent, inventory of work in progress declined to minimal levels, and lead times for deliveries in many industries decreased to a matter of days. Machines that could be reprogrammed could switch to a different product simply with loading of a different program. As a result, competitiveness was determined by the quality of the firm's software rather than by its installed hardware.

Computers are moving into all phases of the production process because of miniaturization, mass production, decreasing costs, and parallel advances in software applications. The power of the mainframe systems of the 1970s was transferred into tabletop workstations in the 1980s and into Pentium-III personal computers in the late 1990s. The units became more and more interconnected through a variety of methods and programs. Distributed computing environments allowed individuals to reach out from their personal computers to networks and special-purpose computers. By the late 1990s, computers had entered every facet of our lives through a product range extending from networking stations, handheld, notebook, laptop, and desktop computers, to multifunction cellular phones, videoconferencing products, automobile navigation systems, and pager network interfaces for e-mail via Ether.

Cognitive processes are being progressively transferred to computers. The storage and processing of information by means of computers and the new technologies of tele-communication are producing vast networks that gather, process, store, and transfer information without requiring or even allowing operational intervention by humans. Such systems are becoming deeply embedded in the functioning of the contemporary corporation and interact with it in count-less ways. Because in many instances control is transferred almost entirely to computers, modern information-processing systems acquire increasing autonomy. Multinational manu-facturing companies are increasingly completely delegating their financial routines to computer programs integrated within worldwide telecommunication networks. Quasiau-tonomous information-processing systems are thoroughly integrated in manufacturing (CIM), design (computer-assisted drafting), and inventory control Just-In-Time (JIT). In many instances these systems have become sine qua non, and the option to switch to human substitutes is no longer a pos-sibility without inducing process down time, dramatically higher costs, and lower productivity.

Information has become the crucial factor in channeling the flow of capital. According to Walter Wriston, long-time head of Citicorp Bank, the information standard has replaced the dollar and gold standards as the basis for international finance. Worldwide communication enables and ensures that money moves anywhere around the globe in answer to the latest information on market variations from expected equilibria.

Since the mid 1970s, there has been an estimated tenfold decrease in unit costs every five years for the same perfor-mance level. A Pentium-III personal computer thus costs ten thousand times less than an IBM mainframe in 1975 and has comparable computing power. The trend is showing no signs of leveling off, suggesting that continued diffusion of infor-mation processing systems in the workplace can be expected. A new nervous system is evolving in industry. It integrates technological systems and human beings with complex mutual feedback loops. It stores information in ways that are far more permanent and several dimensions larger than any form of information storage used in previous business activities.

The Internet is the most powerful and visible technological development in the field of information technology. It has gone from being the exclusive province of computer scientists and university users in the late 1980s to being a primary route of information exchange for everyone from school children to large corporations. There were more than thirty-five millions hosts and 1.3 million servers in 1998. Electronic mail and even videoconferencing are widespread in industry but represent only a small part of the capability of the World Wide Web to store, analyze, and communicate. The Internet is fast becoming an all-encompassing repository of human knowledge and an indispensable tool to find everything from an exegesis of *The Canterbury Tales* to stock picks to news about competitors.

The Internet has evolved without direct management through a chaotic mish-mash of information contained in books and papers and raw scientific data, menus, meeting minutes, advertisements, video and audio recordings, and transcripts of interactive conversations. In the late 1990s, computer technology has come to bear most of the responsibility for organizing this information. Software automatically classifies and indexes collections of digital data and compensates for the inability of humans to sort, index, and classify vast amounts of information in short amounts of time. As anyone who has ever surfed the Net knows, these automated tools categorize and retrieve data in a way different from the way people do. Search engines provide uniform and equal access to all information for all users. Although it offers many advantages, this highly democratic system also poses special problems for businesses, including confidentiality, selectivity, relevance, and productivity.

Since the early 1970s advances in information technologies have made for another quantum leap in the sophistication and complexity of the corporation and its operative technologies. This is the shift to knowledge-based technologies. "Every single technology and with it every industry before 1850 was based on experience," wrote Peter Drucker thirty years ago with uncanny prescience about what was to come. "Knowledge, that is, systematic, purposeful, organized information, had almost nothing to do with any of them."[7] The automobile, the airplane, the electrical industry, the pharmaceutical industry, and other modern industries of the early twentieth century evolved out of craftsmanship and experience. In sharp contrast, the emerging industries of the late twentieth century are based on scientific research and integrated systems of knowledge. This is true in industries as diverse as microelectronics, bio- and genetic engineering, artificial intelligence, new materials, waste management, and communication. University-educated knowledge workers are replacing apprentices who sought skills through experience. Process logistics and whole-factory productivity management are replacing the application of labor and material to single mechanisms.

A second facet of the shift to knowledge-based competition comes from a set of advances that occurred outside of what traditionally is called science. These advances were in knowledge integration. They involved configuration and systems in the activities of industry and drew on a broad array of human knowledge across many sciences and even the humanities. Management information systems in industry today are defined as much by their network or systems characteristics and their functional breadth as they are by the hardware or software they use.

Informatization is composed of advances in information-processing capability based on the compaction and integration of computing and storage; of the shift to knowledge-based technological innovation based on the twentieth century sciences of radiation, high-energy quantum physics, physical chemistry, cellular and molecular biology, and symbolic and nonlinear logic; and of advances in knowledge integration and configuration. All three sets of advances have contributed to a new, faster-changing and vastly more complex foundation for corporate innovation and technology development.

THE NEW CORPORATE REALITY

The quantum increase in the pace and amplitude of change driven by the twin motors of globalization and informatization have led to a quantum change in the nature of the business corporation. The power, span, scope, adaptability, responsibility, regulation, sophistication, and risks of the current-day corporation are so different from those associated with a typical firm in which our parents worked that the properties and dynamics have to be thoroughly reconceptualized. The new reality inside the global corporation can be seen to emerge over time along two major axes, as follows:

- The degree of complexity as measured by information content
- Organizational properties arising out of the increased complexity

The degree of complexity can be conceptualized as starting at a given point in time before the twentieth century with operations at the core. By operations, we mean the mechanics of purchasing raw materials, of turning the raw materials into a semifinished or finished product through labor and machines, and distribution and sales. Financial services, trading, mining, and other types of business activities have a central set of operations that uniquely define them.

New degrees of complexity added over time become key to the viability of the corporation. These dimensions include measurement and control metrics; close relations with suppliers, distributors, and competitors; a shared culture and set of values; alliances and partnerships; and a costly interface with ecology and society. Figure A1.1 shows that the defining dimensions of the corporation increase in number over time

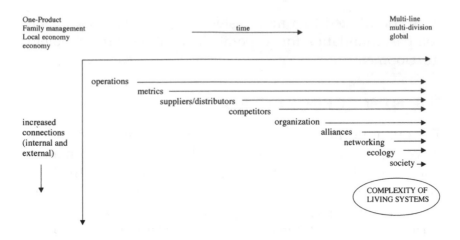

Figure A1.1   Key Dimensions of the Enterprise

and add costly interfaces within and outside the boundaries of the corporation.

The multinational firm of the industrial epoch is largely a static, sum-of-parts, closed and inward-looking entity. It came to be described according to activity structures, hierarchical organizations, shareholding structure, product technology, and quality of management.

THE EMERGING GLOBAL CORPORATION

The complex systems corporation is the next stage, in which the defining properties are less focused on structure and internal resources and more focused on interfaces, relationships, and the dynamics of change. The corporation in this stage becomes an ongoingly self-organizing, open system capable of learning through interaction among employees and between employees and the larger (and no longer strictly outside) world that extends beyond customers, competitors, and suppliers and other classic business partners to the environment and society.

The hallmark of the systemic stage is openness to energy and information flow. The information to which the organization responds includes market, technology, and related direct-business reports and information related to processes in society and the environment. Key elements of the enlarged information base are current and prospective government regulations, competitor practices, industry norms and standards, local community expectations, local and global ecological trends, consumer values, and cross impacts with related industries. The defining properties of this emerging global corporation include the following:

- Learning, self-organization, and nonsummativity: the whole cannot be explained by the parts
- The priority of process over structure: how things change is more important than what they are
- The prevalence of nonlinear probabilistic change: the future can suddenly look nothing like the present
- Fuzzy boundaries: people, departments, and companies are inseparable from their environments
- Heterarchic and networked structures: decentralized multilevel organizations prevail

These properties are drawn from the language and methods of the new sciences of chaos and complexity, which are presented in Chapter 3. Here the key properties are described in conceptual terms. We believe this reconceptualization is valuable to managers, even if it is difficult to relate it directly to day-to-day management. It serves to correct the underlying model with which many managers grew up in microeconomics and business school classes.

What is most interesting is that these five key properties are almost pairwise opposites of the traditional model implicit. Where we identify self-organization, traditional microeconomics postulates no organization and behavioral theory postulates organizational control by senior management. Where we identity fuzzy boundaries, traditional microeconomics asserts well-defined frontiers between the firm and its environment, as does the value-added chain analysis of Michael Porter.

The theoretical construct described in each of the following five key properties of the global corporation presents an altogether different vision of the underlying reality within which managers work.

Learning, Self-organization, and Nonsummativity

Whether at the level of a marketing team, a business unit, or an entire industry, every activity innovates and self-organizes in ways that cannot be reduced to constituent parts. At each point in time the activity is performed differently and involves a different level of complexity. Greater diversity and information intensity emerge. The capacity for each activity to continue learning depends on whether organizational processes and shared values can integrate increased diversity and information flows.

Multidivisional, global corporations develop successful learning cultures (Nordstrom, ABB, Toyota, DHL, Lafarge) or fall into stasis and decline (Wang, Data General, Macy's, Eastern Airlines, Sears Roebuck, Blue Circle). In each case, success or failure cannot be attributed singly or in total to the market, the industry structure, the company's management, or its operations. Instead, auto- and cross-catalytic cycles are useful conceptual devices for explaining self-learning and self-organization as irreducible corporate phenomena.

The Priority of Process over Structure

Flows of material and information in a corporation were seen historically to be determined by the structure of the organization. In matrix models, purchasing, research and development, marketing, and other areas were viewed as stand-alone entities that received the product or service in an unfinished state, added value to it, and delivered it to the next entity. Such structure separation occurred even at very fine levels within manufacturing or services. In dynamically complex enterprises, however, the *processes* of receiving and delivering play a critical role in cost minimization and customer satisfaction. Delays at each level reduce the ability of a firm to deliver the product or service competitively. They also increase the time period of the required forecasting. Increased forecasting horizons mean increased errors and higher inventory costs. The availability of sophisticated information technology (computers + telecommunication + software + information stores) allows companies to engineer processes with very short transfer times between activities and to bundle activities so that costs are minimized at the system level.

The Prevalence of Nonlinear Probabilistic Change

The evolution of the state of the corporation is constant but not continuous; it is progressive but not linear. From time to time management has to make crucial decisions, for example, to break into new markets with new products or services, to refinance part or all of the operations, or to reorganize the corporate structure itself. These constitute sudden changes in the corporation's evolutionary trajectory. They are triggered by instabilities and produce phases of chaos. Managing these processes calls for allowing the self-learning potentials inherent in the organization to come into play by developing several small, parallel, well-focused actions, each with some probability of success. One or more of these actions will then nucleate and produce large, enduring benefits. Japanese companies often are cited for managing product innovation strategy in this way.

Fuzzy Boundaries

Because of increasing geographic span, technological innovations, new competitors, and pollution of land, air, and water, corporations find themselves interacting closely with other companies, governments, and the ecosystem. These interactions make it difficult to separate the interests of the company from those of its operating environment. Noncompliance with ecology legislation and regulation leads to fines, loss of permits, lawsuits and in some cases prison sentences for individual managers. Development of ecology-linked products and services, however, may lead to increased sales, increased stock valuation, and decreased government regulation. The corporation finds itself progressively integrated and a part of its physical environment. A growing parallel trend exists between the corporation and society through its interactions with culture, education, and other quality-of-life factors. Within the business realm, mergers, acquisitions, strategic partnerships, informal networks, minority shareholding, and other modes of interaction between the corporation and other players are effacing the distinction between the company and its competitive environment. The results of these multiactor or multimarket clusters typically are lower unit costs or more profitable price levels due to scale, simplification, pooled resources, and industry rationalization.

Community-based and Networked Structures

Early in the industrial revolution the corporation was typically family based with the founding father, his sons, hired managers, and labor in rigid power relations to each other. As organizations became more sophisticated and diversified, such hierarchies (whether they were single or matrix) proved inadequate to handle the complexity of the business in an information-efficient manner. The artificially imposed structure of the management organization no longer corresponded to the higher level flows of energy and information in a dynamically complex environment. One response to corporations with such hierarchic organizations has been to network functions around specific goals. In an attempt to bypass the formal structure of the organization and accomplish customer-driven product modification, a design engineer may find himself or herself working for a marketing manager in a division with which he or she has no hierarchical ties. A second response has been to flatten organizations and shift staff positions to operational responsibility. Hierarchy flattening tends to save payroll costs and increase information efficiency and responsiveness between leadership and the front-line employees. Both networking and flattening provide companies with a flexibility and competence lacking in formal structures.

The next level of organization is multilevel community-based structures. These provide vertical autonomy because tasks are allocated across the organization and, thus, are more fluid (see principle VIII). Labor, machines, and networks remain specialized, but tasks are performed in a way that optimizes the activity of the organization as a whole. The role of senior management becomes primarily that of facilitator—to coordinate and integrate the functions of the subsidiary levels within the framework of a coherent overall strategy.

The evolution of the corporation and its environment holds true for individual corporation as well as for the corporation as historical entity. As in biology, in which ontogeny recapitulates phylogeny (the development of the individual organism from its inception to maturity repeats the basic phases of the evolution of the species itself), the evolution of the individual enterprise repeats the pattern traced by the evolution of corporations through history. In the business world, as in the living world, evolutionary trends steer developmental processes along analogous pathways. Chapter 3 provides a better understanding of the dynamics involved. Such understanding is essential to comprehending and ultimately to applying a more relevant set of management principles.

Appendix 2

Chaos Models in Business: Notes for the Technically Minded

Technically the term *chaos* refers to a particular state of complex systems. Complex systems that operate in states of chaos range from the world's financial markets to weather over the Pacific Ocean and the human heart during fatal arrhythmia. Business thinkers increasingly are coming to see large-scale organizations as examples of such systems. In states of chaos, they share the following behavior:

1. The time path of the system never repeats itself; it is neither stable nor periodic. Knowledge of the system at a point in time, including the history of the system, will not help us understand how the system will evolve in the future. The trajectory of the system appears random and erratic;

2. The system has sensitive dependence on initial conditions. This means that extremely small difference in parameter values (for example, a change in the unloading sequence in the delivery of raw materials in a highly complex manufacturing network) can lead to widely divergent outcomes (the company achieves global industry leadership or remains an unprofitable secondary player); and

3. There is order and coherence to the time path or sequence of states of the system. A visual mapping

of complex systems in states of chaos reveals that the sequence of states is far from random and that the system's time path does have boundaries.

The last characteristic appears to contradict the first two. Complex systems in states of chaos are simultaneously unpredictable and orderly. Because *chaos* does not mean arbitrariness and disorder, business thinkers are increasingly drawn to modeling business and market systems that exhibit behavior that can only be described as chaotic.

Economists have been interested in modeling complex dynamics for more than half a century, beginning with the work of Frisch (1933), Lundberg (1937), and Samuelson (1939), who used difference equations, differential equations, and mixed models to generate deterministic time paths. A mathematical example of the simplest sort, given by Baumol and Benhabib,[1] is the first-order linear equation, as follows:

$$y_1 = ay_0, \; y_2 = ay_1 = a_2y_0, \; \text{or} \; y_t = a_ty_0$$

Any negative value of parameter *a* results in an oscillatory time path. The primary applications of such models were in macroeconomics rather than the microeconomics of the business firm. As far as complex systems modeling was concerned, it became clear that such linear models were capable of generating only four types of time paths, as follows:

1. Oscillatory and stable (converging with oscillations of decreasing amplitude toward some fixed equilibrium value)
2. Oscillatory and explosive (cycles of ever-increasing amplitude)
3. Nonoscillatory and stable
4. Nonoscillatory and explosive

None of these four linear variants proved useful to modeling systems in states of chaos. It was not until the application of nonlinear mathematical models that economics was able to model complex cycles with irregularities that begin to simulate chaos. Even with the advent of nonlinear mathematical modeling, economists tended to concern themselves with cyclical time paths rather than oscillatory time paths. By cyclical, we mean a time path, y_t, characterized by a cycle the duration of which is p periods if it always replicates itself *precisely* every p periods from any initial point in its trajectory. This is contrasted to an oscillatory time path, which is defined more vaguely as one having frequent rises and declines in the values of its variables but in which the time path may rarely or never replicate an earlier point of its trajectory. The latter nonlinear modeling can yield extremely complex time paths and simulate chaos. Intertemporal behavior can acquire an appearance of disturbance by random shocks and can undergo violent, abrupt qualitative changes, either with the passage of time or with small changes in parameters.

Chaotic time paths can have the following attributes, among others:

- A time path can sometimes display sharp qualitative changes in behavior that appear to be random or erratic.
- A trajectory is sometimes extremely sensitive to microscopic changes in the values of the parameters. A change, say, in the fifth decimal place of one of the parameters can completely transform the qualitative character of the trajectory.
- The trajectory may never return to *any* point it has previously traversed but displays in a bounded region an oscillatory pattern that is consequently highly unpredictable. In other words, the system's time path is simultaneously unpredictable and orderly.

The following simple, nonlinear, one-variable difference equation of the first order provides a feel for chaos dynamics by showing with mathematical precision the extreme sensitivity of complex systems to small changes in parameter values:

$$y_{t+1} = f(y_t) = wy_t (1-y_t), \text{ where } dy_{t+1}/dy = w(1-2y_t)$$

A phase diagram shows values of the time path (the sequence of states of the system over time) for a value of $w = 3.5$. There are four general cases for the corresponding phase diagram, as follows:

1. If $w < 1$ the phase curve will lie entirely below the 45-degree ray, but if $w > 1$ there will be an intersection point E between the phase trajectory and the 45-degree line.
2. In particular, if $1 < w < 2$, the slope of the phase curve at the intersection point will be positive.
3. If $2 < w < 3$, that slope will be negative but between 0 and -1.
4. If $w > 3$, the slope will be less than -1.

It is the fourth variant ($w > 3$) that is of interest to chaos phenomena. In the phase diagram, such a mapped trajectory will be explosive for low initial values of y, and there will be cobweb-like oscillations around point E. At the point at which the trajectory encounters the negative slope of the diagram, the oscillations "explode." As soon as the positive slope is encountered, the oscillations "dampen." For the parametric value $w = 3.5$, these oscillations will involve a rise and a fall in every two successive periods.

A chaos-type trajectory is generated when the value of w is increased to the critical point at which an infinite number of cycle lengths is generated. To see this, we begin with the value $w = 3$. It is *exactly* at this point that the equilibrium point E becomes unstable, because the slope of the phase curve is <

−1. Exactly at that value of w the stable two-period limit cycle becomes observable.

As w increases further (to $w = 3.4495$ in this case), a stable four-period cycle makes its appearance. Further increases in the value of w lead to an infinite number of cycle lengths. The result is an oscillatory time path with no stable cycle (i.e., repeating) period. Chaos behavior is thus approximated from this simple mathematical equation by varying one parameter value over a critical threshold.

An important matter, especially for forecasting purposes, is the sensitivity of such functions to initial conditions. That is, two time paths with similar initial points can give rise to radically divergent outcomes. For example, in the two cases $w = 3.935$ and $w = 3.94$ the time paths beginning from the identical values for y_0 lead to totally unrecognizable phase diagrams after thirty periods.

The consequences for economics of chaos dynamics in complex systems have been to make forecasting extremely difficult. Basic forecasting methods of extrapolation have become ineffective in the following situations:

- A time path might be oscillatory and predictable for thirty periods, the oscillations all but disappearing for the next thirty periods and an explosive n-period cycle emerging abruptly thereafter.
- An error in calculation of the fifth decimal place of a parameter can change the time path of the system (and therefore of the forecast) beyond all recognition.

Economists and the business gurus who have built on quantitative approaches in economics have responded by trying to increase the sophistication of their models. By adding more variables, more equations, and more data and by increasing processing speed they have sought to understand the evolution of large complex systems in all their detail and with maximum predictability. In one amusing commentary on this search for detail, Baumol and Benhabib said that approaches to modeling chaos with applied time series "are complicated by the fact that the data sets used in reality are necessarily finite."[2] This search for detail has been an impossible task at the extremes of a global system that comprises corporations, customers, suppliers, distributors, regional economies, and global ecosystems. Not even the largest Cray supercomputer could cope with the myriad reactions and interactions the search involves. On a purely methodological level, observers (cf., Philip Mirowski in "From Mandelbrot to Chaos in Economic Theory")[3] argue that chaos modeling is intrinsically incapable of the deterministic, law-like outcomes sought through conventional economics. They argue that chaos models are inherently stochastic and blur the distinctions between randomness and determinism and between order and disorder. Therefore, they contradict the very heart and soul of the economist's world view.

Chaos theory and bifurcation dynamics are important theoretical contributions to classic economic and business theories. As systems thinker David Loye emphasized, these conceptual innovations offer a clearer understanding of what happens, can happen, and can be made to happen in a time of turbulent change and mounting economic, corporate, and environmental crises and transformations.

The features of evolutionary systems theory presented in Chapter 3, can help us to understand the context in which corporations operate by providing insight into the dynamics of instability, or more precisely the dynamics of the periodically destabilizing evolutionary process.

LIMITATIONS OF CHAOS MODELING IN ECONOMIC THEORY

Since the early 1980s, an increasing number of academic economists have turned to developments in the new sciences on which evolutionary systems theory is based, in particular chaos theory. These include Baumol and Benhabib in the article cited earlier, Brock ("Distinguishing Random and

Deterministic Systems"), Day ("The Emergence of Chaos from Classical Economic Growth"), and Philip Mirowski ("From Mandelbrot to Chaos in Economic Theory").

The intense attraction that chaos literature exerts on conventional economics is apparent in the history of economic theory. According to Mirowski

> Mathematical economics is essentially coextensive with the school of neo-classical economic theory; and neo-classical theory was directly copied from mid-19th century energy physics. . . . Physics continued to evolve rapidly after the mid-19th century, whereas the neo-classical research program tended to remain mired in its original 19th century orientation. In particular, from James Clerk Maxwell onwards, physics increasingly began to incorporate stochastic ideas into physical explanations, whereas neo-classical economics did not."[4]

In an attempt to go beyond determinism and to catch up with physics as exemplar, economics has begun to investigate models and applications of complexity and chaos theories. Thus far the results have been disappointing. This is in part because the gap between the neo-classicists and the complexity and chaos theorists is so large that bridging it would require wholesale rejection of standard economic thinking and methods. Scale invariance (from the theory of fractals) suggests that the marshallian distinction between the short run and the long run is an analytic mistake. Systemic discontinuity and functions that are nowhere differentiable (such as Weierstrass functions and Cantor dusts) put into question the entire set of methodological tools used in marginalism and in the determination of equilibria. The very concept of efficient markets is threatened. In the conventional economics of the market, arbitrage serves to stabilize prices closer to the underlying equilibrium of supply and demand. Chaos dynamics suggests that there exists a class of important cases in which useful arbitrage is impossible because of discontinuity and explosive change. "The upshot [of complexity and chaos theory] is that almost every technique of orthodox econometrics is useless and would probably have to be discarded," wrote Mirowski.[5]

Baumol and Benhabib are more muted on the disappointing results. They observed that one of the most promising roles of chaos theory is

> revealing sources of uncertainty, and enriching the list of recognized possible developments. . . . Chaos theory has at least equal power in providing caveats for both the economic analyst and the policy designer. For example, it warns us that apparently random behavior may not be random at all. It demonstrates dramatically the dangers of extrapolation and the difficulties that can beset economic forecasting generally. . . . It offers additional insights about the economic sources of oscillations in a number of economic models."[6]

We add that these insights provide equal caution to business leaders, strategists, and planners who fall into one of two classic traps in forecasting, as follows:

- Dismissing complex market behavior as lacking order or believing that the future is random or arbitrary
- Predicting the future with any degree of certainty or planning for the future with single-scenario approaches that necessitate that the organization carry out a sequence of predetermined steps

While admitting that the search for useful chaos models in economic theory has been filled with challenges, Baumol and Benhabib give one simple case applied to the theory of the firm.[7] The case involves the dynamic relation between a firm's profits and its advertising budget. The firm cannot sell anything without some advertising expenditure. As advertising spending rises, total net profit first increases then gradually levels off and finally begins to decline. If Pt represents profits in period t, and yt is the total advertising expenditure, Pt can be taken to have the function $Pt = ayt(1 - yt)$. It is also assumed that the firm devotes a fixed proportion, b, of its current profit to advertising outlays in the following period so that $yt + 1 = bPt$.

For some set of values for a and b, we begin to get oscillations. Even if an increase in advertising outlay raises total revenue, after a point the marginal net profit yield becomes negative thereby reducing advertising outlay in the next period and raising net profit. The increase in net profit increases the advertising outlay in the subsequent period, and so on ad infinitum. This oscillatory pattern "does not give us any reason to expect that these timepaths need either be convergent or perfectly replicatory."[8] In other words, a chaos pattern can be seen to arise.

The new sciences of complexity and chaos have met with only partial and muted success in economic theory and business applications. It remains questionable whether the transposition is at all possible or whether this is an instance in which it would be better to throw out the baby with the bath water, that is, whether economics is at the threshold of a paradigm shift. Nevertheless, as Baumol and Benhabib observed,[9] the influence of the new sciences already introduces a new frame of reference and awareness of the "contours of change" exhibited by complex phenomena. This frame of reference will help theorists and practitioners alike in dealing with the observable world.

Notes

Chapter 4

1. Peter Keen, *The Process Edge* (Boston, MA: Harvard Business School Press, 1997).
2. Daniel Isenberg, *Harvard Business Review* (November–December 1984): 81–90.

Chapter 5

1. Norman Augustine, "Reshaping an Industry: Lockheed Martin's Survival Story," *Harvard Business Review* (May–June 1997): 84.
2. Gary Hamel and C.K. Prahalad, "Corporate Imagination and Expeditionary Marketing," *Harvard Business Review* (July–August 1991). See also their article "The Core Competence of the Corporation," *Harvard Business Review* (May–June 1990).

Chapter 7

1. Kenichi Ohmae, *The Mind of the Strategist* (New York: Penguin Books, 1983).

Chapter 8

1. Andrew Grove, *Only the Paranoid Survive* (New York: Doubleday Currency, 1996).
2. George S. Day, "Strategies for Surviving a Shakeout," *Harvard Business Review* (March–April 1997).

Chapter 11

1. R. Hardy and R. Schwartz, *The Self-Defeating Organization* (Reading, MA: Addison-Wesley, 1996).
2. Henry Mintzberg, "Une journée dans la vie d'un dirigeant," *Revue Française de Gestion* (November–December 1996).
3. *The Economist*, 12 April 1997, 63.

Chapter 14

1. Peter Senge, *The Fifth Discipline* (New York: Doubleday, 1990), 343.
2. Charles Handy, *The Age of Unreason* (Boston: Harvard Business School Press, 1990), 124.

Chapter 16

1. Robert Shapiro, "Growth through Global Sustainability," *Harvard Business Review* (January–February 1997).
2. World Business Council for Sustainable Development (WBCSD), *Environmental Performance and Shareholder Value* (WBCSD, 1997).
3. Yamashita, Sen, and Roberts, in *Environmental Performance and Shareholder Value*.
4. Rachel Carlson, *Silent Spring* (New York: Houghton Mifflin, 1962), 194.
5. Paul Hawken, *The Ecology of Commerce* (New York: HarperBusiness, 1993).
6. Peter Keen, *The Process Edge* (Boston, MA: Harvard Business School Press, 1997).
7. For some of this material, we are indebted to Stuart L. Hart, "Beyond Greening: Strategies for a Sustainable World," *Harvard Business Review* (January–February 1997).
8. *New York Herald Tribune*, April 21, 1997.
9. The authors are indebted to authors of *Environmental Performance and Shareholder Value* for this example and others in this section.
10. *Wall Street Journal*, March 25, 1997.

Appendix 1

1. C. Laszlo, "Emergent Properties and Principles of Management of Multinational Companies," Ph.D. diss., University of Paris X, 1995, Microfilm.

2. Quoted in John Case, *The Open-Book Experience* (Reading, MA: Addison-Wesley, 1998).
3. Joan Magretta, "Growth through Global Sustainability: An Interview with Monsanto's CEO, Robert Shapiro," *Harvard Business Review* (January–February 1997).
4. Charles Handy, *The Age of Paradox* (Boston, MA: Harvard Business School Press, 1990).
5. Securities Data Corp.
6. George S. Day, "Strategies for Surviving a Shakeout," *Harvard Business Review* (March–April 1997).
7. Peter Drucker, *The Age of Discontinuity: Guidelines to Our Changing Society* (New York: Harper Torchbooks, 1968).

Appendix 2

1. William Baumol and Jess Benhabib, "Chaos: Significance, Mechanism, and Economic Applications," *Journal of Economic Perspectives* (Winter 1989): 102.
2. *Ibid.*
3. Philip Mirowski, "From Mandelbrot to Chaos in Economic Theory," paper, University of Notre Dame, 1990.
4. *Ibid.*, 290.
5. *Ibid.*, 297.
6. Baumol and Benhabib, "Chaos," 8.
7. *Ibid.*
8. *Ibid.*
9. *Ibid.*

Index

A

Ackers, John, 52
Act early, 71–72
Action
  concrete guidelines to, 36–38
  tie information to, 153
Activity, build flexibility and
    reactivity into every, 48–49
Adaptive systems approach, 25
Addressograph-Multigraph
    Corporation, 70
Aeroquip Corporation, 177
Age of Paradox, The (Handy), 192
Age of Unreason, The (Handy), 125
Agencies, travel, 140
Ambitions
  communicating timeless, 90–91
  developing, 87–91
    four key actions, 89–91
    greater than means, 87–91
  drive top-down, 89–90
  maintain overriding, 59–60
American Airlines, 140
American LIVES Inc., 168
Analog Devices, Inc., 124, 154
Apple Computer, 50
Artificial intelligence, 108–9
Assumptions of what works,
    continually question, 51–53
AT&T, 9

B

Babson College, 127
Banking industry, 13–14
Benz, Jacques, 97
Berger, David, 180
Bifurcation and chaos, 28–29
Boss-bossing decision makers, 19
Breakdown, avoid, 76–77

Breakthrough, use conflict as source
    of, 128
British Airways, 119
British Petroleum, 129, 180
Browne, John, 129
Business
  chaos models in, 213–21
  design information flows that
      serve, 147–49
  globalization of, 197
  shift in environmental
      responsibility, 163–66
Business and science, bridging gap
    between, 3–4
Business decisions, social
    consequences of global,
    179–80
Business unit, defining, 47–48
Business world, centralization
    and decentralization in, 94–
    95

C

Canterbury Tales, The (Chaucer),
    203
Capital, information and channeling
    flow of, 202
Carson, Rachel, 163–64
Cash flow accounts, modification of,
    169–71
Cash flow statements, 81–84
  continuation of pre-1989 industry
      structure, 83
  create probability-based, 81–84
  in Eastern Europe, 82
  overcapacity and cutthroat
      competition, 83
  rapid Westernization, 82
  revisiting, 168–69

Centralization
  in business world, 94–95
  of operations, 108
Change in living systems
  pattern of, 26–29
    bifurcation and chaos, 28–29
    complexity and convergence,
      27–28
    innovation, 26–27
Changes
  depth of, 36
  factors underlying successful,
    19–21
  pace of, 167–68
  prevalence of nonlinear
    probabilistic, 209
  rhythm of, 36–37
  speed and complexity of, 1
  taking place, 120–21
  turbulent, 21
  unexpected and unpredictable,
    188–89
Chaos
  dynamics
    consequences for economics of,
      217
    lessons from new sciences,
      23–34
    new sciences of complexity and,
      221
  and bifurcation, 28–29
  defined, 23
  dynamics, 23–34
Chaos models
  in business, 213–21
  in economic theory, 218–21
  search for useful, 220
Chaos-type trajectory, 216–17
Chaotic, part of everyday lexicon, 1
Chaotic time paths, attributes of, 215
CIM (computer-integrated
    manufacturing), 200–202
Citicorp Bank, 145, 202
Clarity in organizational structures,
  112
Client companies, value-added offer
  and target, 12

Client-server, 9
Coffee, Starbucks, 50
Cohen, Alex, 127
Coherence, maintain explicit, 84–85
  among finance, 84–85
  among implementation, 84–85
  among organization, 84–85
  among strategy, 84–85
Coherent decision-making systems,
  104
Coke, 136
Collomb, Bertrand, 178
Command and control, 123–30
Communications
  across hierarchical lines, 112–13
  increase to all parts of
    organization, 76
Community-based organizations,
  depend heavily on
  information flows, 113
Community-based structures, 210–
  11
  defining, 111
  strategies developed in, 110
Community-based systems,
  managing, 109–10
Companies; *See also* Corporations;
    Firms
  characteristics of large, 24
  competitive environments of, 118
  complex entities in unstable
    environments of large, 24
  European, 71–72
  information systems in insurance,
    148
  operating on some principles, 41
  pursuing perpetual
    transformation, 87–88
  self-organization in, 30–31
  value-added offer and target
    client, 12
Company standards, establish codes
  of, 67–68
Compensation and performance
  objectives, link between, 103–
  5
Competence; *See* Multicompetence

Competition
  shift to knowledge based, 204
  for sustainability, 64
  sustainable, 66
Competitive environment of
  companies, 118
Competitors, extending partnerships
  with, 66
Complex systems, structuring role
  of, 132
Complexity
  and chaos, 221
  and convergence, 27–28
  defined, 23
  increase of, 151–52
  and instability, 38
Compressors, refrigerator, 44–45
Computers, moving into all phases
  of production process, 201
Conflict, use as source of
  breakthrough, 128
Conflicting viewpoints, encouraging,
  119
Conglomerates, large, 83
Consolidation, industrial, 167
Consumer goods industry, 13, 134–39
  factors for success in, 136–37
    delivered cost, 137
    distributor relations, 136–37
    resource management of
      diversity, 137
    time to market, 136
  future industry operating model,
    139
  leading-edge information flows in,
    138–39
  past information flows in, 135
  use of information technology to
    create dynamic partnerships,
    137–38
Continual repositioning, 55–56
Continuous discontinuity, 188
Contradictions, corporate-life, 190–92
Convergence and complexity, 27–28
Corporate behavior, establish codes
  of, 67–68
Corporate-life contradictions, 190–92

Corporate reality, new, 187–211
  emerging global corporation, 206–
    11
  globalization, 193–94
  industry consolidation, 195–97
  information flow, 194–95
  informatization, 199–205
  span of power of global
    corporations, 198–99
Corporations; *See also* Companies;
  Firms
  complex global, 31
  emerging global, 206–11
  future of, 64
  models of, 33–34
  multinational, 110
  rethinking global, 31–34
  span of power of global, 198–99
Corps de métiers, 188
Costs
  delivered, 137
  and opportunities, 66–67
  shared focus on delivered, 19
Credit Lyonnais (French bank), 118
Cross-catalytic cycles, 30–31
  evident both within and between
    corporation, 30
  evolutionary path followed by, 30
Cultural creatives, 168
Culture, traditional managerial, 189
Currency denominations, 145
Customers, 102–3
  identity value added for, 60
Cycles, cross-catalytic, 30–31

D

Data processing, invention of
  computational architecture of
  digital, 200
Database management systems, 9
Day, George S., 69, 154
Day-to-day decision making, 99–
  101
Decentralization in business world,
  94–95
Decision makers, boss-bossing, 19

Decision-making
  capability, 109
  day-to-day, 99–101
  formal and nonperiodic, 96
  formal and periodic, 95–96
  informal, 96–97
  new conditions of operation and, 21
  perpetual transformation not
      analytic or consensual
      exercise in, 184
  risks associated with slow,
      ineffective, 94
  systems, 93–105
    adapting over time, 97–99
    coherent, 104
    designing, 93–105, 99–105, 93–
      105
  types of, 95–97
Deep Blue, 95
Delivered cost, 137
Dell, 70
Design information flows that serve
    business, 147–49
Development, approach inflection
    points as opportunities for,
    73–75
Digital data processing, invention of
    computational architecture of,
    200
Discontinuity, continuous, 188
Disorder, avoid, 76–77
Distributor relations, 136–37
Diversity, resource management of,
    137
Doing, learn by, 103
Dominant mode, 98
Downsizing, 85–86
Drucker, Peter, 107–8, 204
Dynamic nonstable equilibrium
    defined, 150
Dynamics, chaos, 23–34
Dysfunctional marketing
    information systems, 152

E

Ecological interdependence, 180

Ecological stress, 165
Economic theory, limitations of
    chaos modeling in, 218–21
Economists, interested in modeling
    complex dynamics, 214
Economy, subsistence, 171
Electricité de France, 71
Electrolux, 116–17
Ellison, Larry, 9–10, 50
Employees, exchanges between top
    management and, 101
Environmental action at Lafarge,
    178–79
Environmental drivers, 166–68
  changing value systems, 168
  industrial consolidation, 167
  IT (information technology), 167
  pace of change, 167–68
  population growth, 166–67
  quantifying, 169–70
Environmental issues and financial
    performance, 161–63
Environmental policy, carefully
    articulated, 162
Environmental responsibility, 163–
    66
  shift from government to big
    business, 163–66
Environmental solutions to existing
    problems, 177–81
Environmental sustainability, 159–81
  defined, 160
  extension of Ten Principles, 159–
    81
  our planet is at stake, 171–74
  quantified, 168–69
Equilibrium, dynamic nonstable, 150
European companies, 71–72
EVA (economic value added), 79
Events, recognize potential key, 71–
    72
Evolution defined, 23
Evolutionary influence, 123–30
Exchange
  information, 101
  medium of, 144–45
Expand mode, 98

F

Failures, publicize individual
    successes and, 118
Fifth Discipline, The (Senge), 124
Financial performance,
    environmental issues and,
    161–63
Firms
    See also Companies; Corporations
    traditional multinational, 31
Ford, 41
Formulation, strategy, 11
Front-line operations, 102–3
Future, create future from, 49–50
Future industry operating model, 139
Future not possible, striving for, 89
Fuzzy boundaries, 210

G

Gates, Bill, 9
General Electric Co., 44–45, 119
General Motors, 2, 82
Gerstner, Lou, 52–53, 119
Global business decisions, social
    consequences of, 179–80
Global corporations
    complex, 31
    defining properties, 207
    emerging, 206–11
        community-based and
            networked structures, 210–11
        fuzzy boundaries, 210
        learning, 208
        nonsummativity, 208
        prevalence of nonlinear
            probabilistic change, 209
        priority of process over structure,
            208–9
        self-organization, 208
    rethinking, 31–34
    span of power of, 198–99
Globalization, 193–94
    advent of, 192–93
    of business, 197
    of industrial enterprises, 196
    and informatization, 192–93

Goss, Tracy, 127
Grove, Andrew, 69, 74–75
Growth
    population, 166–67
    strategies, 85–86

H

Handy, Charles, 125, 192
Hart, Stuart L., 160
Harvard Business Review, 41, 69, 190
Hatsopoulos, George, 104
Headquarters
    interfacing with world, 17
    limiting role of, 99–101
    roles of world, 100
Hierarchical lines, facilitating
    communication across, 112–13
Human systems, 24

I

IBM, 41, 52–53, 119, 144
    case of dysfunctional marketing
        information systems, 152
    computer Deep Blue, 95
IBRD (International Bank for
    Reconstruction and
    Development), 170
Identity
    four key actions, 59–62
    maintain long-term, 55–62
    need for long-term, 56–59
    value added for customers, 60
Impossible, be willing to take on,
    127–28
Industrial consolidation, 167
Industrial enterprises, globalization
    of, 196
Industry
    anticipate needs of, 67–68
    banking, 13–14
    consumer goods, 13, 134–39
    oil and gas, 14–15
    pharmaceutical, 14
Industry clustering
    diamond of, 65
    self-supporting, 30

Industry consolidation, 195–97
Industry-level costs and
    opportunities, internalize,
    66–67
Industry operating model, future, 139
Industry sustainability
  compete for, 63–68
  three key actions, 66–68
Inflection points
  approach as opportunities for
    development, 73–75
  create when radical change is
    needed, 75–76
  five key actions, 71–77
  use strategic, 69–77
Influence, creating work
    environment of mutual, 128
Information
  avoiding one-way flows of, 150–51
  channeling flow of capital, 202
  defined, 131
  exchanges, 101
  focusing on relevance of, 149–50
  managing, 131–57
    key to successful
      implementation, 131–57
    seven key actions, 147–57
  nonmaterial nature of, 144–45
  structuring role of, 132
  tie to action, 153
  using to stimulate learning, 153–55
Information flow, 194–95
  community-based organizations
    depend heavily on, 113
  facilitating, 112–13
  openness to, 32
  structure, 155–57
  that serves business, 147–49
Information interfaces, increasing
    number of, 151–52
Information management, key
    actions in, 146–47
Information processing technologies,
    innovations in, 199
Information systems
  case of dysfunctional marketing,
    152

  in insurance companies, 148
  and transformation, 131
Information technologies, 131, 137–
    38, 167
  advances in, 203–4
  as catalyst of process of
    transformation, 133–34
  Internet and, 203
Information technologies; *See* IT
    (information technologies)
  advances in, 203–4
  Internet has become powerful
    technological development in,
    203
Informatization, 199–205
  and globalization, 192–93
Innovation, 26–27
Instability
  intrinsic nature of complexity and,
    38
  and stress, 117
Instability in jobs, avoiding, 116–17
Insurance companies, information
    systems in, 148
Intel Corporation, 69, 73–75
Intel Inside, 74
Intelligence, artificial, 108–9
Intent, strategic, 89
Interdependence, ecological and
    social, 180
Internet
  evolved without direct
    management, 203
  new technologies, 142–45
  powerful development in
    information technology, 203
  represents technological
    discontinuity with past, 144
  Sabre now accessible on, 140
Isenberg, Daniel, 41
ISI (Industry Solution Initiative), 12
IT (information technologies), 131,
    137–38, 167
  advances in, 203–4
  as catalyst of process of
    transformation, 133–34
  Internet and, 203

J

Jackson, Michael, 136
JIT (Just-In-Time), 202
Jobs
  avoiding instability in, 116–17
  avoiding tension in, 116–17

K

Kao Corporation, 126
Kasparov, Gary, 95
Kasriel, Bernard, 117
Keen, Peter, 36, 171
Knowledge based competition, shift
    to, 204
Kombinats defined, 83
Kvaerner, 177

L

Lafarge
  environmental action at, 178–79
  perpetual transformation in action,
    7–8
Lafarge Corporation, 41, 71
  became more open and outward
    looking, 17
  design and dissemination of
    effective reports, 21
  efforts to execute effective change
    had failed, 15–16
  factors underlying successful
    change, 19–21
  forcing of turbulent change from
    within organization, 21
  implementation of information
    and measurement system, 20
  interfacing with world
    headquarters, 17
  large-scale change in capital-
    intensive manufacturing
    business, 15–21
  new conditions of operation and
    decision making, 21
  perpetual transformation
    approach, 16–17
  results after two years, 18–19
  search for big maneuvers, 16

  shared focus on delivered costs, 19
  southern division of, 15
Lafarge Corporation (U.S.), cement
    division of, 7–8
Lafarge S.A., 7–8
  building materials company, 15
Lane, Ray, 10
Large companies
  characteristics of, 24
  complex entities in unstable
    environments, 24
*Last Word On Power, The: Executive
    Reinvention for Leaders Who
    Must Make the Impossible
    Happen* (Goss), 127
Leadership
  based on living-systems model of
    organization, 26
  models drawn from science, 24–
    29
  new approach, 184
Leading, reenvision, 123–30
  four key actions, 127–30
Learn by doing, 103
Learning, 208
  catalyze, 115–21
  using information to stimulate,
    153–55
Lima, Ohio, 180
Living systems, pattern of change in,
    26
Lockheed Marietta, 86
London Perret Roche Group, The,
    127
Long-term identity, need for, 56–59
Lotus, software company, 53
Loye, David, 218
Lucent Technologies, 41

M

Magic Mountain, The (Mann), 184
Management
  Internet evolved without direct,
    203
  key actions in information, 146–47
  reports and metrics, 120

Management gurus, writings, 116
Managerial culture, traditional, 189
Managers, perceive beginnings of
        instability and change, 72
Mann, Thomas, 184
Manufacturing business, large-scale
        change in capital-intensive,
        15–21
Market, time to, 136
Marketing information systems,
        dysfunctional, 152
Marketing, mass, 145–46
Marshall, Colin, 119
Maruta, Yoshio, 126
Mass marketing becomes possible,
        individualized, 145–46
Metrics
    and management reports, 120
    providing clear set of, 120–21
Microsoft, 9, 50
Mintzberg, Henry, 97
Mode
    dominant, 98
    expand, 98
    pioneer, 97–98, 103
    turnaround, 98
Model, future industry operating,
        139
Monsanto, 160, 190
Moore, Gordon, 74
Multicompetence teams, 102–3
Multinational corporations, 110
Multinational firms, traditional, 31
Multiplex Corporation, 155–56

N

National firms; *See* Multinational
        firms
Networked structures, 210–11
Neumann, John von, 200
New science, arena of, 3
Newton, Sir Isaac, 25
Newtonian-cartesian perspective,
        24–25
Nonstable equilibrium, dynamic,
        150

Nonsummativity, 208
Nordstrom's, 72

O

Objectives, meeting specific, 111
Objectives, producing shared vision
        of, 119–20
Oil and gas industry, 14–15
Only the Paranoid Survive (Grove), 75
OPEC (Organization of Petroleum
        Exporting Countries), 47
Operating model, future industry,
        139
Operating units, increasing
        accountability of, 103–5
Operations
    centralization of, 108
    front-line, 102–3
Opportunities, internalize industry-
        level costs and, 66–67
Oracle, 7–15, 50, 144
    approach to perpetual
        transformation, 11–13
    culture of perpetual
        transformation, 8
    global leader in database
        management systems, 9
    industrial expansion and financial
        performance of, 10
    industry-specific approaches, 13–
        15
        banking industry, 13–14
        consumer goods industry, 13
        oil and gas industry, 14–15
        pharmaceutical industry, 14
    managing high-performance
        growth, 8–15
    one of world's largest software
        producers, 9
    stock market performance of, 10
    strategy formulation, 11
    transformation process undertaken
        by, 12
Oracle Corporation, 7
Organization
    adaptation and survival of, 2

for Economic Cooperation and
Development, 134
increase communications to all
parts of, 76
leadership based on living-systems,
26
self, 93–105
turbulent change from within, 21
virtual, 146
Organizational instability, 115–21
five key actions, 117–21
Organizational structures
fluidify, 107–13
lack of clarity in, 112
three key actions, 110–13

P

Partnerships
extending with competitors, 66
mutually beneficial, 65
strategic, 64–65
use of information technology to
create dynamic, 137–38
Penalty avoidance, 174–75
Pepsi, 136
Performance objectives, link between
compensation and, 103–5
Perpetual transformation, 4–6
in action, 7–8
approach, 16–17
companies pursuing, 87–88
culture of, 8
embodied by Ten Principles, 183
essence of, 5
not analytic or consensual exercise
in decision making, 184
not one-time effort, 91
Oracle approach to, 11–13
process of, 155–57
Perret, Solange, 127
Peyrelevade, Jean, 118
Pharmaceutical industry, 14
Pioneer mode, 97–98, 103
Planetary limits, 172
Population growth, 166–67
Porter, Michael, 65

Positioning; *See also* Repositioning
producers reevaluating strategic,
134–35
strategic, 55
Principles, Ten, 35–41
Proactive strategy formulation, 11
Problems, environmental solutions
to existing, 177–81
Process over structure, priority of,
208–9
Procter & Gamble, 133, 144
Producers, reevaluating strategic
positioning, 134–35
Product life-cycle sustainability,
176
Production processes
computers moving into all phases
of, 201
eliminating nonsustainable
practices in, 175–76
Profit, capture defensible, 60–61

R

Rallying cry, developing simple and
recognizable, 90
Ray, Paul H., 168
RDBMS (relational database
management systems), 9
Refrigerator compressors, 44–45
Relations, distributor, 136–37
Reports, design and dissemination of
effective, 21
Repositioning, 55–62
continual, 55–56
four key actions, 59–62
maintain long-term identity while,
62
Requisite variety, law of, 151
Resource management of diversity,
137
Restructuring, 85–86
Results, define responsibility for,
112
Revolutionary influence, 123–30
Risks associated with decision
making, 94

Robot, decentralized-learning, 109
Roche, Peter, 127
Royal Dutch/Shell, 46–47

S

Sabre now accessible on Internet,
    140
Scenarios, create what-if, 46–47
Science
    arena of new, 3
    bridging gap between business
        and, 3–4
    models of leadership drawn from,
        24–29
Sciences, advances in new, 2
Seismic-shift syndrome, 69
Self-organization, 93–105, 208
    in companies, 30–31
    defined, 112
    promoting, 93–94
Self-supporting industry cluster, 30
Senge, Peter, 124
Shapiro, Robert, 160, 190
Shared vision of objectives,
        producing, 119–20
Shareholder value creation, 79–86
    link transformation to, 79–86
    three key actions, 81–86
Shareholder value management,
        80–81
    difficulties of implementing, 80–81
Shotoku, Prince, 126
Silent Spring (Carson), 163–64
Singapore, 58–59
Skills, evolving portfolio of, 47–48
Sloan, Alfred, 2, 82
Social interdependence, 180
Software, Lotus, 53
Solutions, environmental, 177–81
Starbucks Coffee, 50
Stata, Ray, 124, 154
Statements, cash flow, 81–84
Strategic intent defined, 89
Strategic partnerships, 64–65
Strategic positioning
    defined, 55

producers reevaluating, 134–35
Strategic tools
    increase use of forward-looking,
        61–62
    mind-set for use of new, 62
Strategies
    create adaptive, 43–53
    five key actions, 46–53
Strategy formulation, 11
    proactive, 11
Stress, 117
    ecological, 165
Structures
    community-based and networked,
        210–11
    priority of process over, 208–9
Subsistence economy, 171
Successes
    and failures, 118
    selectively forgetting past recipes
        for, 51–53
Sustainability
    competition for, 64
    modification of cash flow accounts,
        169–71
Syndrome, seismic-shift, 69
Systems, human, 24

T

Teams, multicompetence, 102–3
Technologies
    new Internet, 142–45
    rate of transformation in, 31
Ten Principles, 35–41
    as concrete guidelines to action,
        36–38
    defined, 39–40
    dynamics involved, 38
    extension of, 159–81
    focus on company transformation,
        159
    integrating, 40
    leading companies operating on
        some of, 41
    not simple recipes or management
        tools, 37–38

perpetual transformation embodied in, 183
synopsis of, 38–40
Tension in jobs, avoiding, 116–17
Thermo Electron, 104
Time to market, 136
Timeless ambitions, communicating, 90–91
Tools
increase use of forward-looking strategic, 61–62
mind-set for use of new strategic, 62
Top management and employees, increase informal exchanges between, 101
Toyota, 144
Transformation
companies pursuing perpetual, 87–88
defined, 5
essence of perpetual, 5
and information systems, 131
IT (information technology) as catalyst of process of, 133–34
not determined by genetic code, 5
perpetual, 4–6
process undertaken by Oracle, 12
rate in technologies, 31
Travel agencies, 140
Travel industry, 140–42
new entrants, 141–42
Trucks, Volvo, 170
Tumultuous, 1
Turnaround mode, 98

U

United Nations, 164
University of Michigan Business School, 160
Unix, 9

V

Value creation
opportunities and sources of, 174–81

eliminating nonsustainable practices in production processes, 175–76
environmental solutions to existing problems, 177–81
penalty avoidance, 174–75
product life-cycle sustainability, 176
Value systems, changing, 168
Variety, law of requisite, 151
View, keeping largest, 129–30
Viewpoints, encouraging conflicting, 119
Virtual organization, 146
Vision, shared, 119–20
Volkswagen, 72
Volvo trucks, 170

W

Wal-Mart, 72, 133
Wall Street Journal, 180
Welch, Jack, 119
Wharton School of Management, 154
What-if scenarios, create, 46–47
Wisdom
new, 1–6
arena of new science, 3
bridging gap between business and science, 3–4
perpetual transformation, 4–6
search for, 1–3
Work environment of mutual influence, creating, 128
World Bank, 170, 173
World Business Council for Sustainable Development, 162
World headquarters
interfacing with, 17
roles of, 100
Wriston, Walter, 145, 202

Y

Yew, Lee Kuan, 58–59